WHAT DO WE TELL THE CHILDREN?

confusion, conflict and complexity

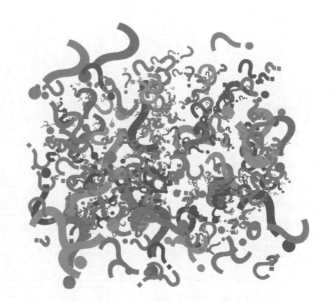

WHAT DO WE TELL THE CHILDREN?
confusion, conflict and complexity

Angela Gluck Wood

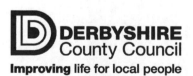
DERBYSHIRE
County Council
Improving life for local people

Trentham Books
Stoke on Trent, UK and Sterling, USA

Trentham Books Limited
Westview House   22883 Quicksilver Drive
734 London Road   Sterling
Oakhill   VA 20166-2012
Stoke on Trent   USA
Staffordshire
England ST4 5NP

First published 2007

British Library Cataloguing-in-Publication Data
A catalogue record for this book is available from the British
Library

ISBN: 978 1 85856 407 4

DISCLAIMER
Every effort has been made to acknowledge the source of all
the illustrations used in this book. However it has proved
impossible to trace a few of them, for which we apologise. If
we receive information about any of those we have omitted,
we will of course include them in reprints of this book.

Designed and typeset by Trentham Print Design Ltd, Chester
and printed in Great Britain by Bemrose Shafron (Printers)
Ltd, Chester

In memory of Ester Gluck
who would know just what to say

Contents

Acknowledgements

This book emerged from a piece of work commissioned by Derbyshire SACRE (Standing Advisory Council for Religious Education) and supported by Derbyshire Local Authority, specifically through the role of SACRE's lead officer, Steve Ford: he is one of the authority's school improvement advisers and has responsibility for religious education, PSHE (personal, social and health education) and education for citizenship. It was a bold and enlightened decision to provide support and advice for teachers in addressing issues of confusion, conflict and complexity. In this, Steve Ford's vision and commitment were paramount.

It was immediately apparent that the needs of Derbyshire teachers are not unique and that the work could helpfully be shared more widely. Thus the partnership with Trentham Books was born. Gillian Klein's alacrity in deciding to publish is probably record-breaking and her enthusiasm remains undiminished.

My friend and colleague at the Insted consultancy, Robin Richardson, provided several well-considered pointers when reading the first draft and for these I am most grateful.

All of the resources and activities in Part III – Craft and Curriculum – have been piloted in a range of classrooms and improved in the light of that experience. My heartfelt thanks go to the teachers and pupils involved for their full and frank feedback – and for the absence of complaints about the inevitable disturbance to their routines!

I pay tribute to my daughter, Ester Gluck. From an early age, she took a keen interest whenever I was 'doing a writing' and increasingly offered perceptive comments and suggestions, based on a close attention to the text that was way beyond any daughterly duty. Characteristically, she brought her wisdom and wit, sensitivity and sharpness to her reading of the first draft of *What do we tell the children?* some two months before her tragic and untimely death in September 2006. Ester was my greatest 'critical friend' – the greatest I could ever hope for.

Introduction

This project could hardly be more timely.

Children and young people are growing up in a complex and confusing world. Part of that complexity and confusion derives from the conflict caused by, or connected to, religious beliefs, political ideologies and philosophical life stances. These conflicts are particularly likely to erupt when two different absolutes meet – or, as is more common, clash. These clashes both stem from and result in a dislike of the unlike, and even outright bigotry. Increasingly, this is expressed in both verbal and physical violence – a violence that makes 'good news'. All religions speak of 'good news' of another order but this voice is often drowned. That billions of believers the world over are neither fundamentalist nor fanatical – but rather desire peace and understanding for themselves and others – is a fact that the media and popular discourse seldom reflect. This compounds the complexity and confusion.

All areas of the curriculum have a part to play in illuminating some of this complexity and dispelling some of this confusion, and religious education (RE) has perhaps the greatest potential role here, for at least two reasons:

- RE is most obviously a vehicle for knowledge and understanding *about religions* (and also sometimes ideologies and other life stances). As such, it is a curriculum area that is well placed to present these positions, as far as is possible, *in their own terms.*
- The material with which RE deals – that is, substance of belief, behaviour and belonging – is not a body of dry facts. Rather they are embedded in and evoke *matters of ultimate meaning and value.* Inevitably, the study of this subject matter gives rise to a range of pupils' responses and has the potential to touch them deep in their lives. RE – as most teachers and coordinators will attest – is often the place where pupils raise life questions whether or not they are on the agenda.

Yet it is clear that many of us feel ill equipped in the area of what might be called 'competing truth claims' and understandably most of us avoid it – perhaps because we have no time, perhaps because we have no resources, perhaps because we had no training...

This book offers preparation for teaching in this area and also a number of specific resources for use in the classroom. These do not constitute a scheme of work but rather provide teaching and learning matter, to be used flexibly in conjunction with existing schemes of study according to your professional judgement as a teacher.

The book is arranged in three main parts:

Part I: CONFLICT AND COMPLEXITY
- pointers to and materials for *preparing yourself* for the confusion, conflict and complexity

These are largely of a generic nature but they also exposes specific forms of bigotry and absolutism in contemporary society, with particular reference to antisemitism and especially to Islamophobia.

Part II: CHARTING A COURSE

■ guidance on approaching issues of confusion, conflict and complexity *in the classroom*

Part III: CRAFT AND CURRICULUM

■ suggested *learning activities and materials*, including stories; text puzzles; black and white line drawings; role play and simulation cards; templates for investigating media reports...

The book includes material and activities applicable to pupils from the Foundation Stage to Year 13, but most of it is particularly relevant to Key Stages 2-4. All the learning activities have been piloted with the relevant age groups.

The title of this book – *What do we tell the children?* – evokes dilemmas about the scope of sensitive matters when we talk with children and young people. It was deliberately chosen to indicate that adults may themselves be uncomfortable and bewildered but realise that children and young people have pressing and pertinent questions – and seek a response even if there is no Answer.

> If we can't promise
> That it will never happen again,
> Or that it won't, if it happens again,
> Happen to them,
> Or that if it does happen again,
> And this time to them,
> We will come save them,
> Or that, if we can't save them,
> Somebody else will,
> Or that, if no one can save them,
> It won't hurt,
> Or it won't hurt that much,
> Or it won't hurt that long,
> Could we tell them
> To please stop asking so many questions?
> *Judith Viorst, on the first anniversary of 9/11*

So indeed, this project could hardly be more timely.

PART I
CONFUSION, CONFLICT AND COMPLEXITY
background and context

☐ No Such Thing as Neutral

☐ Otherising the Other

☐ Mind Your Language

☐ Islamophobia

☐ Antisemitism and Antizionism

■ No such thing as neutral

Pick up a paper: any daily, weekly or monthly; tabloid or broadsheet; local, national or international. For that matter, turn on any radio or television news programme or visit any news website.

Chances are that at least one of the items – perhaps even a leading story – will feature a critical conflict.

Chances are, also, that the conflict item will involve physical violence: a war, terrorist attack, assassination, street disturbance...

Chances are, furthermore, that there will be an element of inter-ethnic hatred or religious bigotry. Perhaps the story operates at a micro level – and is reported as such – but there is almost invariably a macro story of which it is a part, often as a fractal. Perhaps the inter-ethnic hatred and religious bigotry are described as the excuse for the violence, whereas the real cause is a land-grabbing motive or other power struggle. This can mask the reality that religious, ideological and philosophical views are themselves sometimes a source of the conflict, especially where one or more of the groups

involved have a superior or supremacist self-image, that is, where they encourage a dislike of the unlike, where they believe that they hold the Truth and that they have the right to promulgate and impose it.

Such is the world that enters our space, as we travel to work, jog, relax in the armchair or have our breakfast. Such, too, is the world that enters the space of the children and young people we teach, though it may come to them in an even more fragmented way than it does to us, and possibly less directly but rather through the world-views of the adults in their lives.

More even than adults, children and young people are increasingly susceptible to the unregulated medium of the Internet, where there may be no attempt at, or pretence, of neutrality. Indeed, the Internet provides a free forum for the generation of hatred and violence. (The interactive CD-Rom *Digital Terrorism and Hate*, produced in May 2006 by the Simon Wiesenthal Center and the Museum of Tolerance www.wiesenthal.com, identifies 5,000 'problematic sites posted by terrorist, extremist and hate groups worldwide'.)

At one level, we expect and sometimes assume that news reports in the regulated media tell it like it is: our opinion-formation is based on this information. At another level, we know that there may be accidental or deliberate errors, that truth is corrupted by partial and partisan reporting and that there is misinformation, as well as disinformation. We know all about bias and stereotyping. Legend has it that the late Harold Wilson PM once said to members of the Press, 'You shouldn't believe what you write in the papers!'

■ 'Otherising' the Other

> Where is the wisdom we have lost in knowledge?
>
> Where is the knowledge we have lost in information?

wrote T. S. Eliot in the opening Stanza to *Choruses from the Rock*.

We do not read, watch or listen to the news in order to find out about ourselves – although our reactions inevitably remind us of, and even reinforce, our beliefs, our disposition, our hopes, our fears. Rather we wish, ostensibly, to find out about the 'other'. Have they caught that bloke yet? Which side won? Has so-and-so said anything about such-and-such? What was the verdict? Have there been any more bombs? Or simply, what's going on, what's been happening? We want to feel connected to the big world.

Yet often the starkness and simplicity of media presentations of the other – and the sheer speed and volume of them – belie the complexity and subtlety of lives and events that we are lulled into thinking we know and understand. Paradoxically, they are further from – not closer to – our world. They are less than real and not like us.

Education at school can play an influential role in countering any 'otherising' of the other. Like a story-behind-the-story documentary, it can encourage empathy, develop an awareness of diversity, cultivate an appreciation of complexity and prepare the young for living with paradox. It does not need to – and ought not to – push a

particular line, for there are no ratings to raise. Notwithstanding the enormous pressures on busy teachers and the relentless demands of the curriculum, there is none of the urgency, the split-second pace and the instant sound bite of the newsroom. The classroom can be a place of reflection, where children and young people to begin to know, understand and value that which is other and to deal with the doubts that come with openness.

Open and closed

Open and closed views of the other are a running motif of The Parekh Report – *The Future of Multi-Ethnic Britain*. Our society will be happier, healthier and more harmonious, it argues, if we develop open – that is to say, fuller and richer – views of each other. This approach is presented as a chart on page 3.

Outside the box

Two lightly edited personal testimonies appear on pages 4 and 5, both written in 2006, both transcending the news, both exhibiting – though in different ways – an enormous sense of openness and both brave in their willingness to think outside the box. They are offered as potent exemplars. The first focuses on an individual's community in relation to the wider society, the second on an individual's country in relation to another country with which it is in conflict. One is from a Muslim perspective, one from a Jewish. One is analytical, one anecdotal.

The title of the first – 'We don't do God, we do Palestine and Iraq' – (on page 4) is likely to be derived from a remark by Alastair Campbell, Tony Blair's former press secretary. David Margolick's profile of Blair in *Vanity Fair* (May 2003) cited Campbell, when pressed by journalists on the matter of the Prime Minister's faith – the subject of some public interest and mild ridicule – to retort, 'We don't do God!' Amir Tahri, an Iranian journalist writing for the British media, uses the phrase in relation to the politicisation of Islam in a form and for reasons that he laments.

In the second – 'Now the fruit will wait till it rots' (page 5) – Yossi Sarid, living in northern Israel, describes the horrors of armed Hizbollah-Israel conflict from immediate personal experience and reflects empathetically on such an experience for people in south Lebanon. This piece was published in an Israeli daily on the sixth day of the conflict, centred in northern Israel and mostly southern Lebanon. A moshav is a cooperative agricultural settlement that may comprise several small farms. A kibbutz is more akin to a large commune, with pooling of labour and resources and some degree of domestic communality. 'Rotting fruit' is both literal and metaphorical.

OPEN AND CLOSED VIEWS: WAYS OF SEEING THE OTHER

Distinctions	Closed views of the other	Open views of the other
1. Monolithic/diverse	The other is seen as a single monolithic bloc, static and unresponsive to new realities.	The other is seen as diverse and progressive, with internal differences, debates and development.
2. Separate/interacting	The other is seen as separate (a) not having any aims or values in common with the self; (b) not affected by it; (c) not influencing it.	The other is seen as interdependent with the self (a) having certain shared values and aims; (b) affected by it; (c) having an impact on it.
3. Inferior/different	The other is seen as inferior to the self e.g. 'primitive', irrational, 'fundamentalist'.	The other is seen as different but of equal worth.
4. Enemy/partner	The other is seen as violent, aggressive, threatening, to be defeated and perhaps dominated.	The other is seen as an actual or potential partner in joint co-operative enterprises and in the solution of shared problems.
5. Manipulative/sincere	The other is seen as manipulative and deceitful, bent only on their own advantage.	The other is seen as sincere in their beliefs, not hypocritical.
6. Criticisms of the self rejected/considered	Criticisms made by the other of the self are rejected out of hand.	Criticisms of the self by the other are considered and debated.
7. Discrimination defended/criticised	Hostility towards the other is used to justify discriminatory practices and exclusion of the other from mainstream society.	Debates and disagreements with the other do not diminish efforts to combat discrimination and exclusion.
8. Hostility towards the other seen as natural/problematic	Fear and hostility towards the other are accepted as natural and 'normal'.	Critical views of the other are themselves subjected to critique, lest they be inaccurate and unfair.

WE DON'T DO GOD, WE DO PALESTINE AND IRAQ
Amir Tahri, *The Sunday Times*, 12 February 2006

'It looks like a duck, quacks like a duck and flies like a duck. And yet it insists that it is not a duck. This is the image that comes to mind when watching those anti-cartoon marches in western capitals, including London, in the name of Islam.

Isn't Islam supposed to be a religion? Shouldn't it be concerned with the broader issues of human existence...? Today the visible Islam, the loudest Islam, is a political movement masquerading as a religion. Many mosques in this country have been transformed into political clubs where Kashmir, Iraq and Palestine and 'the misdeeds of Anglo-Saxon imperialism' have replaced issues of religious faith as the principal theme... This political Islam also has grievances about aspects of British and more broadly European domestic politics... It is scandalised by the West's 'corruption and debauchery' and that there is no 'moral force' to set strict limits to individual liberties.'

He suggests 'at least three reasons for the excessive politicisation of Islam in the West':

1. Because Muslims in the West are from a wide variety of ethnic, sectarian and cultural backgrounds – often with long histories of feuds in their homelands that cannot continue here – they 'tend to minimise the religious aspects of Islam and emphasise the political themes that can unite them'.

2. The 'public expression of Islam is controlled by political groups and parties that are often banned in the Muslim world itself...' and the West offers 'the only space in which all Islamic political movements can thrive.' Of the more than 400 Islamic associations and societies in Britain operating through some 2,000 mosques, 'scratch any one of them and you will find that it is, in fact, a cover for a political movement... Because it offers a unique freedom, Britain has become host to dozens of Islamist parties which are banned in the Muslim world...groups that could best be described as terrorist outfits have had propaganda bases and safe havens in Britain for two decades.'

3. The politicisation of Islam in Britain is related to its 'rapprochement with the extreme left over the past decade. Today political Islam and the British extreme left are in coalition in a number of organisations... Hatred of 'bourgeois democracy', anti-Americanism and opposition to Israel provide the unifying factors of this unnatural alliance.'

'Islam cannot have it both ways: pretend to be a religion and demand special respect while operating as a political ideology which, by definition, must be open to criticism and even denigration.'

'Politicised Islam's attempt at destroying individual freedoms is as much a threat to Islam as the inquisition was to Christianity. By preaching martyrdom as the highest goal for Muslims and beating the drums of 'the clash of civilisations', it is also a threat to world peace. To protect itself, Islam needs to revive its theology with emphasis on divinity. In other words, Islam must re-become a religion.'

...

'This does not mean that Muslims should stay out of politics or not be concerned about Palestine, Iraq and Kashmir or any political cause.'

'It means they should recognise that those causes are political, not religious. Nobody prevents Muslims practising their faith in Palestine or Kashmir, let alone Iraq. These disputes are about territory, borders, statehood, form of government, not about faith.'

'Politicised Islam is a form of totalitarianism. Its primary victims are Muslims. In many Muslim countries it has been exposed and can no longer deceive the masses. In the West, however, it has duped media, government and academia into treating it not as a political movement, but as a religion.'

'Advocates of politicised Islam claim that a call for Islam to return to God, to resuscitate its dead theology and to re-become a religion is nothing but a 'Zionist-imperialist plot' to divert 'the rage of the Muslim masses'.'

'More Muslims, however, are beginning to miss God, to feel His absence in their religious discourse and to long for His return where He belongs – at the heart of the faith.'

NOW THE FRUIT WILL WAIT TILL IT ROTS
Yossi Sarid, HaAretz, 17 July 2006

'Moshav Margaliot in the north could be called a remote place. I wonder when remote places are most neglected – in war time, or in peace? My impression is that in quiet times they move farther away. No one remembers them, no one is interested in them... Margaliot sits right on the fence , the closest place to the Lebanese border. It is a beautiful place, with breathtaking, little-known beauty. Nothing can equal the magic of the valley below as seen from the mountain.

Moshav Margaliot doesn't complain much, but that doesn't mean it's not deprived. I have to apologise in [that] its name that it doesn't appear on the list of Katyusha-targeted communities. The other side ignores Margaliot too, and won't waste a rocket on it. Not even a dud.

On Friday afternoon it seemed for a moment that the gates of heaven had opened and at last signs of Katyusha were found. We were sitting – Eitan and Liran and Kobi and I – on the balcony overlooking Kiryat Shmona, and without warning Eitan shouted 'Katyusha!' and pushed me into the reinforced room. And indeed we heard a rocket landing below us. I immediately called the mayor of Kiryat Shmona and Haim Barbibai confirmed that rockets had landed, but in an open field, thank God...

On Friday and Saturday nights more Katyusha rockets fell to our right and left, almost all the valley and mountain communities were hit as choppers and planes plowed the sky, but Margaliot was left out. When you listen to the radio and television, remember us: 'the Galilee Panhandle' that's us. Don't forget Margaliot.

Margaliot farmers grow chickens and fruit-peaches, pears, apples, nectarines. The peaches and pears have a life of their own, regardless of the security circumstances. They are rounding out, blushing mildly and awaiting the picking. A delay could cause a whole year's labor and investment to be lost.

So we went out to our orchards near Kibbutz Yiftah to check out the pears...

I lay under a tree, thinking of the fruit that was ripening on the other side of the border as well. I thought of the Lebanese farmers watching their fruit from their window, longing to pick it. I remember them from the time I lived here. On Saturday morning I'd make myself coffee and look out of the open window. They used to stand there on the mountain opposite, looking at me. They'd wave to me and I'd wave back.

They knew who I was; I knew who they were – they were Hezbollah people. In southern Lebanon most people are Hezbollah, whether they want to be or not, and let our prime minister, defense minister and chief of staff make no mistake: They too have families and homes, fields and orchards, apples and pears and chickens. When they used to stand on the mountain on quiet days, looking, waving, shouting – they looked and sounded like human beings look and sound.

Until someone there goes crazy and infects them with his madness; until someone here goes crazy. Now the fruit will wait till it rots.'

COHESION AND INCLUSION IN SCHOOLS

statements referring to Muslim pupils, their families and communities, made by headteachers, governors, teachers and other staff

1. When they're in Qur'an classes, they're not roaming round the streets.

2. Some children, because of their own spirit, will rise above their parents – in spite of their family.

3. Schools are struggling, as it is, to teach what they're meant to, without having to take on relations with the mosque.

4. I can phone the mosque any time to ask for a speaker. I haven't asked since 9/11, though. I didn't think they'd want to come.

5. For Ramadan, we prepare the other pupils so they can support the Muslims and know why they're not in dinners.

6. The girls are more assertive nowadays. They're not shy. They're confident. They don't say, 'Yes Sir, no Sir, three bags full Sir.'

7. I don't agree that all religions and cultures are equal. There are always differences. You can't treat everyone equally, because they're not the same.

8. A very small percentage of governors are Muslim: not enough come forward. It's 'Catch 22': they need to be role models but they have no role models.

9. Muslim boys group together in the playground more than in the past. An outsider might misinterpret this but, if they went closer, they'd hear the boys were discussing cricket.

10. Groups in the community supported the London bombings and there are people who were not at all surprised by the bombs. The school has to show it understands where people are coming from – [to be] and be a place that holds people, lets them know they're understood.

11. A member of staff saw a group of Year 6 Muslim boys talking. 'What are you boys huddling about?' she asked. One of them turned round, looked her straight in the eye – he's a street kid, really sharp – and said, 'Oh, we're just planning the next 9/11, Miss!'

12. We make Eid at school like a mini-Christmas, like Eid in the children's homes. We decorate classrooms, read stories, say prayers, and have fashion shows of Eid clothes, and parties for children and parents. It's for the whole school, not only the Muslim children.

13. I'm not singling out Qur'an classes. Other faith education has things wrong. But we hear some stories about Qur'anic classes – problems with teaching methods and discipline. It's a bit of a taboo area to be saying we're going to look into this but, if there's something wrong, someone has to.

14. I know this is controversial but the mosque has a massive knock-on effect. You can set something up that you know will help them – like a booster class or a sporting thing – but the mosque takes precedence. There's loss of sleep and not doing their homework. The Chair of governors went to talk to the imam.

15. There's a deep sense of shame amongst Muslims and a feeling that all of them are being judged. The school has to be a place where people are allowed to cry and to be angry. Parents want guidance from the school on how they can help their children, particularly their boys, not to go off the rails.

16. They've got a wonderful extended family where they do things together and they go and wave someone off at the airport or go to the hospital *en masse*. There's that aspect of it that other parts of the city haven't got. Where you've got all White inner city areas that are dire, they haven't got that. I understand that and I admire it.

17. The 2$\frac{1}{2}$ hours in the mosque five days a week is precious to them. It helps them think about their actions and it takes their mind off everything. Women in mosque are role models for girls in puberty. The children love the mosque school. We have children crying because they're too young for the mosque classes and they can't go.

18. These children have not just to learn the Qur'an, they've also to live it in their everyday life. I use the Qur'an when talking about their behaviour. Particularly when they're being awful to some other child, I ask them, 'What would the Qur'an say about this? Does the Qur'an say that you can batter someone in the playground?' They say that it doesn't. So I tell them, 'When you're learning the Qur'an of a night, start living it of a day!' Some teachers wouldn't dare use the Qur'an. It's the PC bit.

19. The problem we have is that families understandably want to go back and visit but no one wants to go in the summer holidays, as the fares are high and it's a lot hotter. The extended holidays tend to come around January-February time. I had to say to them, 'Six weeks is a long time for a child to miss school.' Now they know, if they asked for a holiday for that amount of time, I'd say 'No'. So they come to me and say somebody's died or somebody's sick. What can I say? But how is it that, in these families, people only seem to die or are seriously ill when it's cooler and the fares are cheaper? It's a real dilemma.

20. Male members of the community wouldn't shake my hand. I said, 'I know I'm a woman – and, worse than that, a White woman – but in my school, in my office, you have to do things my way. This isn't going to progress unless you treat me equally.' The next time they came they shook my hand. Now we've got really good rapport. A headteacher's a headteacher and Muslim fathers will listen to me, even though I'm a White woman. One of them tried patronising me and I said, 'You're a charmer but you're not charming me. You should spend more time with your son, talking to him, listening to him.' He did and that boy's a changed person since his father started giving him time.

Cohesion and inclusion

Headteachers, governors and staff members in several schools were interviewed on their understanding of cohesion and inclusion, and they volunteered a range of examples. The 20 statements chosen for this collection are all related to Muslim pupils, their families and communities. In our society, Muslim groups and individuals are frequently the subject of closed thinking. However, between them, these 20 statements express open and closed views to varying degrees and, in some cases, within the same statement. They appear on page 6 and are arranged in ascending order of length!

These statements have at least three possible applications in teacher education:

■ assessing the degree of openness in each of the 20 statements against the criteria in the chart, 'Open and closed views of the other' (page 3) so as to clarify understandings of the concept of 'open' and 'closed' *

■ reflecting on the nature of the closed views that are commonly held of Muslims in Britain *

■ considering the implications of cohesion and inclusiveness for the ethos of a school, through the personal and practical examples given

* The first two of these applications might also be relevant as the basis of a learning activity for older pupils.

■ Mind your language

> **Hindu pupil to RE teacher**: I've brought in one of our gods to show you, Ms.
>
> **RE teacher**: Oooh! Thank you. Really beautiful. But don't you mean, um, one of your family's idols... er, that *represents* God?
>
> **Hindu pupil**: Oh no, Ms... Our *God*.

This snippet of dialogue illustrates both the paradoxes and pitfalls that characterise language used to explain, explore and express ideas about religion. The same hold for ideologies and philosophical life-stances.

The pupil and the teacher in this scene are talking about a *murti*. We can only speculate as to why the pupil did not use that term. Did she assume that the non-Hindu RE teacher would not be familiar with it? Or had she become accustomed to translating, as it were, everything Hindu into English, when speaking with non-Hindus? If so, was it to make it more comprehensible to the listener? Less embarrassing for her personally – that is, less 'other'? And what of the RE teacher? She did not use the term '*murti*' in her reply – so perhaps the Hindu pupil was right! But she knows that 'gods' is problematic because polytheism has low status in a society influenced by Christianity. She also seems to have had sufficient exposure to some strands of Hindu thought to be aware of the belief held by possibly the majority of Hindus in 'the One in the many': all 'gods' are manifestations of the one supreme divinity. So she offers the word 'idols' – perhaps to remove or reduce the polytheism – because she is sensitive and caring, has given the Hindu beliefs the benefit of the doubt and wants the Hindu tradition to have high status. But 'idol' is offensive to the Hindu pupil: it implies something artificial, merely a reminder or signpost, not an item infused with deep and layered meanings. 'Idol' has also become humanised, that is, de-divinised. It's to do with football players, pop singers and film stars. A *murti* is not a pinup, literally or metaphorically. 'Idol' just won't do.

All of this, and more, is packed into that 35-word dialogue-including the 'Ooooh', the 'um' and the 'er'!

There are dilemmas deep in many descriptions. Some adult females consider it a compliment to be described as a lady; others an insult. Likewise, there are people who use the term 'coloured' to refer to themselves and eschew 'Black' as an insult because it has negative connotations. (Indeed 'black' does and colloquial English regularly associates misery and evil with the colour black, as in such expressions as 'blackening someone's character' and 'it was a black day.') We might speculate that such people have internalised this negativity or absorbed colonial language forms. Do we respect their personal preference? Or do we insist on the language of reclamation favoured by most because the case needs to be made – even at the risk of insulting some individuals?

Consider the similarities and differences between these three sentences:

A. On 1 September 1939, the Germans invaded Poland.

B. On 1 September 1939, Germany invaded Poland.

C. On 1 September 1939, the Nazis invaded Poland.

All three refer to the same event and all three are factually accurate, given the language in which history is written. Yet through the looseness of language, they tell three different stories:

A. This sentence involves all the people of Germany in the decision to invade Poland and in the invasion itself. While there was tremendous popular support for the Third Reich, including its land-grabbing policies and activities, it is not the case that all Germans were in favour of the invasion and certainly not that all Germans invaded. Aside from the facts of the matter, there are the implications of this wording. Poland is no longer occupied by Germany yet there are Germans today. A sentence such as this indicts them by association.

B. This sentence suggests that the government of Germany ordered the invasion and that the armed forces invaded. It exonerates the citizens. Yet Germany had various forms of support from other countries even at that date and certainly later. In a sense, Germany did not act alone. Yet again, there is a Germany today that is very different from the Germany of 1939: it has had to live through, live with and live down its Nazi past.

C. This sentence bypasses nationality and posits the party as the player. Not all Germans were Nazis and not all Nazis were Germans. Nazis today advocate and sometimes carry out actions that are similar in some respects to those of the German Nazis, from whom they often claim to be 'descendants'.

How should we describe the actors in the invasion of Poland – Germans, Germany or Nazis? How should we describe the actors in the Final Solution – Germans, Germany or Nazis?

In the case of the invasion of Poland, sentence B seems preferable because one polity acted against another polity and it is usual to speak of one country – rather than the citizens of the country or a political party – invading another country. In general, however, it seems preferable to refer to the policies and actions of the Third Reich as Nazi, for all the reasons given under the explanation for sentence C. For example, it is more accurate to speak of the Nazis conducting experiments on Romany children, the Nazis closing down homosexual clubs, the Nazis confining Jews in ghettos, the Nazis operating extermination camps.

With reference to the latter, there is an interesting development in the significance of nomenclature. In 1979 the United Nations designated Auschwitz as a World Heritage site. For years, Poland was incensed by media references to 'Polish concentration camps', implying that Poles were responsible for them. In 2006 Poland urged the United Nations to change 'Auschwitz Concentration Camp' to 'Former Nazi German Concentration Camp of Auschwitz', to make it clear that Nazis rather than Poles were to blame for it. Yad Vashem, Israel's Holocaust Memorial Museum, and other groups endorsed this request. The UN promised a decision in 2007.

Keeping language in order

The sequencing of events – especially in matters of conflict, confusion and complexity – is paramount and it is not always merely an issue of 'who started it'. We seek wholeness and yearn for connections. Our minds make a gestalt, providing us with cause and effect to explain an action or situation. We tend to assume that something that happened after something else was as a result of the something else. This is encapsulated in the Latin term '*post hoc, propter hoc*': after this, because of this.

Consider these two pairs of sentences:

They got drunk.　　　They failed their exam.

They failed their exam.　　　They got drunk.

The words are identical in each pair of sentences but the sequence of sentences is different. Here there is a literal gap between each sentence in the pair and there is also a mental or metaphorical gap. In that gap, we invent a 'because' or a 'therefore', creating entirely different stories that we could read as:

■ **EITHER** They were so inebriated that they could not perform well in the exam.

■ **OR** They were so upset at having done badly in the exam that they consoled themselves with drink.

It follows that, as teachers, we must take care with the sequence in which we present facts and ideas to the pupils and we must also encourage pupils to be ever alert to the order of play in written, spoken and visual material.

Finding the right word

The language field is a minefield. Yet we cannot help setting foot in it because language is the only language we have! We have to say *something*. 'The limits of my language,' said the 20th century linguistic philosopher Ludwig Wittgenstein, 'are the limits of my world.' Language not only communicates meaning: it also makes meaning. That is why we must tiptoe through.

Words change in their meanings and implications over time, and say different things to different people. Changes of language occur partly because the outer world changes, partly because our understanding of the world changes, and partly because various language communities gain greater power and influence and are able to give greater voice to their views. So uncertainties about language are often bound up with changing relationships, and changing patterns of influence and power, in society at large. Concerns in the tabloid press about political correctness, for example, are connected with concerns about social change more widely, not just about language.

'Two countries divided by a common language' – an expression attributed to George Bernard Shaw – describes linguistic differences between the UK and the USA. We might also think of several groups within the UK that are divided by a common language. That is, there are language communities and constituencies that use different English words for the same thing; or use the same English words with entirely different meanings. Language behaviour reveals the beliefs and belonging of the writer or speaker. What we say is who we are. For example, Derry and Londonderry are the same place but the names are used by different communities. So people asking for directions to Londonderry or Derry are revealing not only where they are literally going to but also metaphorically where they are coming from.

There are implications for our language behaviour as teachers in at least four senses:

- by thinking through the likely impact of our word choices, when speaking to and writing for pupils
- by making pupils aware that there are language communities and constituencies, thus enabling them to appreciate part of the texture of language
- by introducing pupils to some of the preferred or determined terminologies of contemporary language communities and constituencies, that they should learn to navigate
- by developing a shared usage with our colleagues

'Finding the right word' (page 11) presents a range of contemporary word choices, through two, three or four words/phrases in each of 30 strips. To describe a particular phenomenon in a given situation, any one of the words/phrases *might* be used: the one that is used reveals something of the identity of the language community or constituency. The question is: what do they reveal?

(The arrangement of words and phrases is alphabetical, both across each strip and also down the 30 strips.)

Some of these sets of words/phrases are very similar in meaning; some are highly nuanced; some may even have oppositional meanings, depending on the speaker/writer and the listener/reader.

'Finding the right word' can be used for individual reflection, or for pair work in a teacher education session or the basis of a learning activity for older pupils. A discussion of these clusters of words and phrases appears as 'The answers at the back of the book' on pages 121-128.

Two points of special focus appear here (as sections D and E) that might be considered as a special form of racism, a sub-set: Islamophobia; and antisemitism and antizionism.

They affect those living in Britain – including school pupils – as well as in other parts of the world. They have been in the news for a considerable time and, by all accounts, are likely to remain there in the foreseeable future. From time to time, they are the subject of public enquiry and occasionally of outcry.

Pupils might be victims, perpetrators, bystanders or rescuers. In any event, they are likely to encounter these phenomena sooner or later, if they have not done so already.

There is no special pleading here and certainly no numbers game: the arithmetic of suffering is invidious. Rather, these two phenomena are chosen for reasons of their confusion and complexity.

FINDING THE RIGHT WORD

| African Caribbean | Afro-Caribbean | Black British | West Indian |

anti-Muslim racism — Islamophobia

anti-Judaism — antisemitism — anti-zionism

arranged marriage — assisted marriage — forced marriage

assimilation — integration

coloured people — people of colour

community cohesion — social inclusion

conservative — fundamentalist

disturbances — riots

diversity — equality

ethnic minority — minority ethnic

extremist — fanatical — radical

faith — religion — spirituality

Falklands — Malvinas

freedom-fighter — insurgent — militant — terrorist

gender — sex

Global South — Third World

god — God

Gypsy — Romany — Traveller

idol — image — symbol

Indian sub-continent — South Asia

interfaith — multifaith

Islamic — Islamist — Muslim

Israel — Israel-Palestine — Palestine

lady — woman

political correctness — political correctness gone mad

pupils with special needs — SEN pupils

racial — racist

resistance — revolt — revolution

you — you people

■ Islamophobia

Although Islamophobia may literally mean a fear of Islam, the term is generally used to mean hatred of or opposition to Islam. In practice, it manifests as hatred of Muslims. It has a long history, dating in Europe from the 8th century – almost from the inception of the Islamic community. Because it can take many forms and focus on varying elements of Islamic culture, it is probably more accurate to speak of *Islamophobias.*

In Britain, alongside numerous articles and individual reports, there have been two major published studies of the phenomenon of Islamophobia, each resulting in recommendations for change made to authorities, social institutions and the media. The second study – *Islamophobia: issues, challenges and action* – was produced in 2004 by the Commission on British Muslims and Islamophobia. Both versions contain vision statements reminiscent of the 'I have a dream'

speech of Martin Luther King Jr. An extract from the 2004 version appears in the box below.

The eight points in the 'our vision' statement express ideals, which are the flipside, as it were, of elements of the reality experienced by Muslims in British society.

These two exercises might provide an element of teacher education in an understanding of Islamophobia or, most effectively, form the basis of learning activities for older pupils by:

■ summarising each of the eight points of 'our vision' with a short phrase.

■ reconstructing the reality experienced by Muslims in British society – a reality that is in contradistinction to the ideals expressed in 'Our vision'.

'Most people living in what we still loosely call the west would agree that we do have troubles with Islam,' wrote Timothy Garton Ash (*The Guardian*, 15 September 2005). 'The vast majority of Muslims are not terrorists, but most

---

Our vision

The day will come when:

1. British Muslims participate fully and confidently at all levels in the political, cultural, social and economic life of the country.

2. The voices of British Muslims are fully heard and held in the same respect as the voices of other communities and groups. Their individual and collective contributions to wider society are acknowledged and celebrated, locally, regionally and nationally.

3. Islamophobic behaviour is recognised as unacceptable and is no longer tolerated in public. Whenever it occurs, people in positions of leadership and influence speak out and condemn it.

4. Legal sanctions against religious discrimination in employment and service delivery are on the statute book and offences aggravated by religious hostility are dealt with severely.

5. The state system of education includes a number of Muslim schools, and all mainstream state schools provide effectively for the pastoral, religious and cultural needs of their Muslim pupils. The range of academic attainment amongst Muslim pupils and students is the same as for the country generally.

6. The need of young British Muslims to develop their religious and cultural identity in a British context is accepted and supported.

7. Measures to tackle social and economic deprivation, unemployment and neighbourhood renewal are of benefit to Muslims as to all other communities.

8. All employers and service providers ensure that, in addition to compliance with legal requirements on non-discrimination, they demonstrate high regard for religious, cultural and ethnic diversity.

of the terrorists who threaten us claim to be Muslims. Most countries with a Muslim majority show a resistance to what Europeans and Americans generally view as desirable modernity, including the essentials of liberal democracy.'

Garton Ash seems to suggest that Islam and the West have no points of commonality and thus are essentially other to one another – an idea reinforced by 'us' and 'ourselves'. However, the ideas of interaction and reflection emerge from the title of his article: *What we call Islam is a mirror in which we see ourselves.* He posits – with some critical and constructive comments – six views of Islam, that is, six possible attitudes to Islam that an individual or a society might adopt. More to the point, these views reveal more about the characteristics of the viewer than of the viewed. In other words, Islam reveals 'us' to 'ourselves'. It is as though we create Islam in our own image. Garton Ash's six views are summarised in the box opposite.

Garton Ash concludes, 'Now, which of the six views got your largest tick? In answering that question, you will not just be saying something about the Islamic world; you will be saying something about yourself. For what we call Islam is a mirror in which we see ourselves. Tell me your Islam and I will tell you who you are.'

Garton Ash's invitation to discriminate and prioritise offers a stimulating and challenging exercise. More demanding still – and equally valid – would be an exploration of possible responses to these six views. Both are appropriate for teacher education and the possible basis of learning activities for older pupils.

They might profitably lead to a consideration of the following two samples from young British Muslim culture. Neither is suggested as 'typical' but both defy stereotypes.

WHAT'S THE NUB OF THE PROBLEM?

1. **Religion**
   Religion itself – all religion – is problematic because it is based on superstition. Society would do better to rely on the findings of science and the application of reason.

2. **Islam**
   Islam does not allow 'the separation of religion and politics'. Further, it retains outdated and unreformed attitudes to such matters as gender equality and homosexuality, and its system of punishment is 'barbaric'.

3. **Islamism**
   Islam has become distorted by 'fanatics' and used as a 'political ideology of hate'.

4. **Arabs**
   Most Arab countries have Muslim majorities and few have democratic forms of government. They have not modernised their institutions in the post-colonial period.

5. **Christian and post-Christian societies**
   Dominant Christian and post-Christian ideologies have – by their behaviour – made enemies of Islamic societies. Such behaviour includes the creation of the State of Israel.

6. **Tensions in encounter**
   Direct contact between first or second generation young Muslims in Britain and secular consumerist society causes either frustration at the failure to succeed within it or repulsion at its values. Their experience of marginalisation creates a sense of alienation and, for some, an involvement in extreme action.

GAME OF POOL

This photograph, chosen to accompany Judith Bumpus' article, 'Saudis see how their sisters live' (*The Times*, 10 May 2006), was part of a series about Shopna and her friends, taken by Suki Dhanda in 2002.

In *Only Half of Me: being a Muslim in Britain* (2006), journalist Rageh Omaar describes an event on a double-decker London bus. He was sitting on the lower deck and suddenly became aware of eight teenage schoolgirls clattering and tumbling down from the top deck, shouting to each other or on their mobile phones, and full of gaiety and laughter. They were from a range of backgrounds, including Somali. Omaar writes:

> The Somali girls switched back and forth, in and out, from a thick London accent to Somali. One of them turned to her white friend and screeched, 'Those bacon crisps are disgusting! Just keep that minging smell away from me girl, I tell ya!' and then fell about laughing. They discussed each other's clothes and another girl in their class, then one of the Somali girls shouted, 'Bisinka! did you really say that?' In one breath she went from a Somali Muslim word, Bisinka, which means 'By God's Mercy' or 'With God's help', and which Somalis say when something shocking happens, to English. None of her friends, black, white or Muslim, batted an eyelid.

■ Antisemitism and Anti-zionism

Technically, 'antisemitism' is a misnomer as there is no such thing as 'semitism'. There are Semitic languages – which include Arabic as well as Hebrew. However, antisemitism is not hatred of a group of languages but hatred of a group of people; and it refers to vilification of Jews, not of Arabs. Yet the term, which was coined in 1879, has stuck.

Antisemitism has a long history and has been especially prevalent in the Christian world, although in this context it might more properly be described as anti-Judaism. With the advent of modernity – that is, in the 18th century – which began to see a decline in the authority of the Church, antisemitism has persisted within secular frameworks. In the 20th century, there have been expressions of antisemitism emanating from some parts of the Islamic world. Whereas in the past, political antisemitism has come from the far right, the term 'new antisemitism' has been coined to refer to its relatively recent manifestation on the far left, sometimes in collaboration with Islamist groups. In 1994, The Runnymede Trust produced a report on the patterns of antisemitism in Britain. It drew its title – *A Very Light Sleeper* – from Conor Cruise O'Brien's comment about antisemitism – and was subtitled the *persistence and dangers of antisemitism.*

In September 2006 the All Party Parliamentary Inquiry into Antisemitism was published. It documented the resurgence of verbal and physical antisemitism in Britain since 2000. It coined the term 'antisemitic discourse' to describe the widespread change of tone in which Jews are discussed by others in private and in public and noted that such discourse exists across the political spectrum.

Christian antisemitism – an example in a particular form

Views about Jews and Judaism are central to the traditional Christian message. No other religion in the world has ever attached such significance to its attitude towards, and treatment of, another specific religious tradition. Classic Christian antisemitism has particular implications for RE teachers because its source is in the New Testament, aspects of which feature prominently in the RE curriculum.

The classic view is that Jews rejected Jesus as the Messiah and they represent the old and unredeemed order: for this reason the Jewish Bible which forms part of the Christian Bible is called 'The Old Testament'. The Christian tradition has also taught that Jews instigated Jesus' death, and this charge of deicide is linked to the Christian beliefs that God has rejected the Jewish people and the Church had replaced them: today this is dubbed 'replacement theology'. Although physical attacks by Christians against Jews were widespread in the Middle Ages, the official view was that Jews should be encouraged or forced to convert to Christianity. Failing that, they should be caused to suffer yet preferably preserved as a reminder of the 'Old' and a warning about the fate that would befall doubters, detractors and defectors.

This subtle and complex message was encapsulated in a particular motif in Christian art: Ecclesia and Synagoga (church and synagogue) figures. They are female forms that appear side by side as a pair. Ecclesia appears on the right, from God's point of view, as it were, and Synagoga on the left: symbolically, right is 'good' and left is 'bad'. From our viewpoint, though, their positions are reversed.

Window of St. John's Church in Werben Elbe River, Germany c. 1414-1467

Ecclesia is riding a four-formed creature – with the heads of an eagle, a human, a lion and a bull – symbolising the four Gospels. She is holding a flag, with a cross on the top of the staff, and an uplifted chalice. The divine hand from heaven places a crown on her head.

Synagoga is riding a donkey, which seems about to collapse. In her right hand she holds the head of a he-goat, symbol of the devil. Her crown is falling. She is blindfolded. The staff of her flag is broken. The divine hand from heaven pierces her head with the sword of judgment.

In many forms of Ecclesia and Synagoga, the two women are very similar – almost identical twins, at least sisters. It is their clothes and accessories – religious artefacts – as well as their body language, that marks them apart. This has great symbolic value because clothes and accessories can be acquired, and body language can be adopted. It is as though the church is telling the Jews that their weakness and inferiority are not intrinsic; Christian strength and superiority can be acquired and adopted through conversion.

The specific items in and features of this image need some unpacking and decoding – whether in teacher education sessions or lessons for older pupils. The notes on either side of the image are useful in this respect but much can also be inferred through close observation and intuition. It is valuable as an educational exercise to develop skills to read an image.

Antisemitism – and – Antizionism

Antizionism is hatred of Israel or opposition to Zionism, which derives from Mount Zion, the hill on which the city of Jerusalem was built. Zion became and remains synonymous with Jerusalem in Jewish prayers and songs, and symbolises holiness.

There are at least four main reasons for confusion and complexity in relation to antisemitism and antizionism:

■ Being a Jew is not necessarily, and is not only, a matter of religion. In the modern period, it is valid to speak of secular Jews. Jews have been described as a racial group but this is inaccurate. It is more appropriate to speak of the Jewish people.

■ Classic Christian anti-Judaism derives from two Christian theological views: firstly, that Jews were responsible for deicide – literally, killing God – in demanding the crucifixion of Jesus; and secondly, that Christianity has superceded Judaism. Classic Christian anti-Judaism has travelled worldwide through the spread of Christianity. It manifests as antisemitism even in places where Christians have no experience of Jews living amongst them. From the 20th century, there have been Christian scholars, clergy and lay people willing to revisit the theological basis of antisemitism as well as others resistant to such a revisiting.

■ The Jewish people is particularly small, with a population of about 13 million worldwide – a figure that is, demographically speaking, less than the margin for error in China. The Jewish people has been threatened with extinction more than once in its history.

Zionism as a religious, cultural and political movement has several meanings, including: the return to the biblical and ancestral homeland from which the Jews were exiled; the fulfilment of a duty to settle the land and make it flourish; the establishment of the Jewish people's autonomy; the securing of a safe haven for Jews, because of the threat of persecution and annihilation; and the strengthening of Jewish culture and the Jewish people.

Zionism as a modern political movement dates from the late 19th century. In the 1880s, small numbers of Jews made their way from Russia to the Land of Israel, then the region of Palestine in the Ottoman Empire. They were mostly young men and women, fired with progressive and even socialist ideals. They bought plots of land and lived simply, cultivating the soil. Key events in the development of Zionism include:

■ The **Zionist Congress**, convened in 1897, which aimed to establish a home for the Jewish people in the Land of Israel, secured under public law

■ The **Balfour Declaration** in 1917, which stated, 'His Majesty's Government view with favour the establishment in Palestine of a national home for the Jewish people, and will use their best endeavours to facilitate the achievement of this object...'

■ The **British Mandate of Palestine** in the aftermath of World War I, when the Ottoman Empire ended

■ The **United Nations Partition Plan** of 1947, which proposed dividing Palestine into an Arab and a Jewish State

■ The **creation of the State of Israel** in 1948

■ There are substantial links and overlaps between antisemitism and antizionism, because Israel is a Jewish state – the only Jewish state – and the overwhelming majority of Jews support its right to exist, with security.

In recent years, attention has been focused on possible links between antisemitism and antizionism. In one sense, a relationship would be entirely natural because Israel is the homeland of the Jewish people. But it is not so simple, and the issues are highly nuanced and intricately textured. It is full of paradoxes and ironies. Furthermore, antisemitism – and – antizionism has spawned some alliances of political parties or organisations that are otherwise poles apart. Despite all this complexity, it is possible to tease out the strands a little and to discern a number of positions, three of which appear below:

One: Antizionism is antisemitism

■ There are some who hate Jews and hate Israel, and do not differentiate between them or their hatred of them.

■ The corollary is that there are Jews inside Israel and throughout the world who have such a strong sense of common history and common destiny that they experience the hatred directed at the other as hatred directed at them. More than that, they share a view, based on an ancient Hebrew saying, that all Jews should be responsible for one another.

■ Some Christian leaders and groups, who are positive towards Jews and Israel, also interpret antizionism as a form of antisemitism.

Two: Antisemitism and antizionism are entirely distinct

■ There are those who believe that hatred of Jews as *Jews* is unjustifiable. However, they find hatred of Israel totally justifiable – and it comes in what might be termed strong and weak versions. It is the singling out of Israel for vilification – among all the nations of the world – that constitutes antizionism.

■ The **strong** version is opposed to the very idea of a Jewish state *as a Jewish state*, which it deems to be neo-colonialist or racist. In this connection, often referred to is the resolution of the General Assembly of the United Nations in 1975 that 'Zionism is a form of racism'. Seldom referred to is the fact that in 1991 that resolution was revoked by a larger majority.

■ The **weak** version takes issue with particular actions or policies of the Israeli government but not with similar – or more reprehensible – actions or policies of other countries.

■ A very small number of Jews (outside Israel) opt for the **strong** version. It is likely that they have both distanced themselves from the Jewish community – thus otherising it – and have adopted political leanings to the far left, thus sharing the inherited view of 'Jewish world conspiracy' in some form.

■ A small number of Jews outside Israel align themselves with the **weak** version. They are probably more numerous than those who adopt the strong version. Nevertheless, they remain very much a minority within the Jewish community. Some of them stand in the age-old and much honoured Jewish tradition of self-criticism: as an extension, this includes criticism of one's community or society. Further, there are Jews who distance themselves from the actions and policies of the Israeli government critics within Israel because they resent, as it were, being guilty by association in a climate of hostility towards Israel.

Three: Antizionism is a cover for antisemitism

■ When there is criticism of Israel and it is met with counter criticism, the critics of Israel sometimes claim that they are being stifled by Israel's supporters and feel threatened with the charge of antisemitism.

■ As a corollary, there is a growing sense – amongst Jewish groups, some Christian friends and others – that ostensible antizionism derives from and is fuelled by classic antisemitism because antisemitic language, imagery and action would provoke a counter-claim of racism. They note, for example, that:

☐ 'Jews', 'Zionists' and 'Israel' are frequently used interchangeably.

☐ In visual representations (such as cartoons), Jewish imagery and medieval stereotypes of Jews are chosen to represent Israel.

☐ False claims against Jews – such as blood libels – are revived.

☐ In particular, the blatantly antisemitic *The Protocols of the Learned Elders of Zion* (first published in 1897) is frequently republished and widely distributed; in some countries there are film versions shown on television.

■ For Jews, Christians and others who are alert to these phenomena, antizionism and antisemitism are identical in effect, even if not by intention.

The 3 Ds

An important contribution to the clarification of possible relationships between antisemitism and antizionism was provided by Natan Sharansky in a speech given at the OSCE (Organisation for Security and Co-operation in Europe) conference on antisemitism in Berlin in 2004, at which he was the head of the Israeli Delegation. He referred to the 'resurgence of anti Semitic activity specifically on the continent of Europe' and posited '3Ds': **demonisation; double standards; delegitimisation**. A lightly edited extract from his speech appears in the box.

'We are sometimes blamed for trying to stop the legitimate criticism of Israel by accusing our opponents of antisemitism... Israel as the only genuine democracy in the Middle East enjoys a robust and public ongoing political debate. Israel welcomes criticism like every robust democracy both from in and without.

But where is the line between legitimate criticism of Israel and antisemitism? We must have a clear standard for defining this line... I call it the 3D test. This test... takes the same criteria that for centuries identified the different dimensions of classical antisemitism and applies them to the new antisemitism.'

The first D is the test of demonization
'That was the main instrument of antisemitism against Jews. Jews were accused of drinking the blood of children, spoiling the wells, controlling the banks and governments.' He refers to a film on blood libels as 'most primitive and crude... (it) reaches the homes of tens of millions instantly as well as millions of homes in Europe. The most vicious persistent and genocidal forms of antisemitism now emanate from radical theological elements in the Muslim world...'

Citing the words of a foremost Saudi cleric, he says, 'This terminology of antisemitism is very dangerous – but at least very easy to identify. Today, the most sophisticated form of demonization is demonization of the Jewish State. For example, the comparisons of Israelis to Nazis and of the Palestinian refugee camps to Auschwitz... can only be considered antisemitic... even those who seek to place the blame on Israel cannot legitimately compare these camps to Auschwitz... This is a clearcut case of demonization.'

The second D is the test of double standard
'For thousands of years, a clear sign of antisemitism was treating Jews differently than other peoples, from the discriminatory laws that many nations enacted against them

to the tendency to judge their behavior by a different yardstick. Similarly, today we must ask whether criticism of Israel is being applied selectively. If Israel, the only democracy in the Middle East, is condemned by the Human Rights Commission for the violation of human rights more than all the many dictatorial regimes existing over the past 50 years together, it means that a different yardstick is used towards Israel than towards other countries. And a different yardstick means a double standard and a double standard means antisemitism.'

The third D is the test of delegitimization

'In the past, anti-Semites tried to deny the legitimacy of the Jewish religion, the Jewish people or both. Today, they are trying to deny the legitimacy of the Jewish State. While criticism of an Israeli policy may not be antisemitic, the denial of Israel's right to exist is always antisemitic.

Like a pair of glasses in a 3D movie that allows us to see everything with perfect clarity, the 3D test I have proposed will allow us to see antisemitism clearly and therefore enable us to fight it more effectively.'

The crystal – clarity of the 3Ds makes it an effective template for an examination of the effect on other religious, cultural or ideological groups of the hostility that they experience. For example, might the 3Ds template fit the experiences of people seeking asylum in Britain?

With a group of colleagues – or in a classroom of older pupils – take the criteria of Sharansky's 3D test and apply them to a different religious, cultural or ideological group – locally, nationally or internationally.

- What are the effects on that group of demonization, a double standard and delegitimization?
- How might those effects be mitigated?

■ The Good, the Bad and the Untidy

In *Outside Edge*, a British television sitcom series based around an amateur cricket club, the team captain was irritatingly punctilious, obsessed with routine, and intolerant of indiscipline and disarray. He hated unpredictability, liked to be in control and had an imperious manner. In one episode, a player challenged him with: 'Chaos is the law of nature; order is the dream of man.'

Describing chaos as law seems a contradiction in terms. We usually understand laws as antidotes to chaos, as guiding forces that order society and our individual lives. Yet perhaps the world is not chaotic but has its own structure and rhythm that we cannot know; and perhaps it is our own sense of chaos, when events seems random and experiences seem meaningless, that makes us impose order on the natural world and human relationships, in a way that is satisfying and strengthening.

In his poem The Cool Web, Robert Graves writes of the paradox of order and chaos, and the central image is of language. As children, he says, we are close to the heart of things and in touch with emotion, but unable to express what we feel. Words help us manage what we experience but also have the effect of dulling our sensations and narrowing the scope of our experience. Yet, paradoxically, to be fully human we cannot live without language; if we did, he says, we would die.

...

But if we let our tongues loose self-possession,
Throwing off language and its watery clasp
Before our death, instead of when death comes,
Facing the wide glare of the children's day,
Facing the rose, the dark sky and the drums,
We shall go mad no doubt and die that way.

As with language, so it is with religions, ideologies and philosophical life-stances. They make sense of reality and contain it so that we are not overwhelmed. They point us to the ultimate but also protect us from it. They both inspire us with lore and yet constrain us with law. Their essence is neither entirely law nor entirely lore: the interrelationship between law and lore is at its heart. Law without lore is dead. Lore without law is wild.

This is not neat and simple, and it is even more untidy and more difficult when religious, ideological and philosophical life-stances are laid side by side, as it were: they are both similar and different. One of the most significant differences lies in the attitudes and behaviours that a tradition or system adopts towards other traditions and systems. It's about otherness. Traditions and systems occupy the whole spectrum:

■ a claim to hold the absolute truth from which others – who are inferior and otherised – are excluded...

■ a claim to hold the absolute truth which others are invited – or pressured or even forced – to accept...

■ an open door that others can either take or leave...

■ a conviction that no one has the Truth but that all have a truth...

■ and all stations in between.

A key skill in teaching and learning is therefore the ability to 'read' religions, ideologies and life-stances so as to discern which is where on this continuum – and why.

This **C-R-E-A-D** structure (in box) may support this 'reading' of creeds and suggest a number of approaches – and their downsides – that we might take in education and in public discourse:

These three approaches to religion feature prominently among those adopted by adherents of religious traditions (and sometimes others) in contemporary Western society. They are:

■ Fundamentalism

■ The search for shared values

■ Dialogue

C **Competing truth claims**

We can see some religions, ideologies and life-stances as being like advertising pitches, all claiming to have authority, to be 'it'.

■ BUT they cannot all be ultimately true. So either only one of them is or none of them is.

R **Relativity**

With a range of religions, ideologies and life-stances, everything is relative. There's no right and wrong. We can pick any one – or none.

■ BUT if religions, ideologies and life-stances are pointers to the ultimate, one of them has to be the Truth.

E **'Equivalencing'**

Religions, ideologies and life-stances all look the same to us. A feature in one (such as a festival of light) has its equivalent in another.

■ BUT these are similarities only in form. The forms have different meanings and so we cannot 'equivalence'.

A **Absolute truth**

Some religions, ideologies and life-stances are confident that they have – or are – the one Truth. This gives their members a lot of confidence, too.

■ BUT they cannot prove they are true. Anyway, absolute beliefs create a false sense of superiority, which leads to a dislike of the unlike...

D **Diversity**

Life is rich and varied. We are richer when we appreciate this variety. Society is more just when we are committed to faith equality.

■ BUT people need to be rooted, earthed, connected to something strong and secure.

The three approaches are outlined below (pages 21-23) and each matches one or more elements of the C-R-E-A-D structure. A task to match a given approach to elements of the C-R-E-A-D structure would form the basis of a profitable teacher education session or lesson for older pupils.

Fundamentalism

Fundamentalism today is a feature of more than one religious or ideological group. Its strongest and clearest characteristics are delineated as 'Five features of fundamentalism: how fundamentalism thinks and relates to the world' (see the box opposite). It especially relates to religious fundamentalism and is a summary and reordering of Grahame Thompson's article 'What is fundamentalism?'

Frequently So-and-So or Such-and-Such group in the public arena is described as fundamentalist. In the context of a teacher education session or a lesson for older pupils, these five features (opposite) can be used as a checklist to explore the speech and behaviour of So-and-So or Such-and-Such group. This can enhance understanding of the individual or group and can refine understanding of fundamentalism.

The search for shared values: the example of 'The Golden Rule'

A number of projects have been generated to identify what religious traditions have in common, in the hope that it will further joint endeavours and thereby enhance community cohesion. Purists among experts in the study of religions consider this to be artificial because it risks blurring the distinctive identities of the discrete traditions and systems by forcing them into a mould in the interest of finding equivalents and matching apparent similarities.

In the case of the teachings of the world's religious systems about the 'Golden Rule', however, there are striking similarities of wording. Paul McKenna, in a Canadian project, collected such sayings to create 'The Golden Rule Across the World's Religions' poster on page 23.

FIVE FEATURES OF FUNDAMENTALISM: HOW FUNDAMENTALISTS THINK AND RELATE TO THE WORLD

1. **Extremism**
   The most defining characteristic of fundamentalism is its sense of certainty about the beliefs that are held, to the point of totally disregarding alternative viewpoints and those who hold them. Fundamentalists' pursuit of their ideals and principles fosters blind faith and a dismissal of pragmatic reason.

2. **Leader-fixation**
   Extremism is further strengthened when fundamentalists invest their ideals and principles in the figure of a single leader. They are highly deferential towards this leader, whom they are likely to perceive as a saviour figure.

3. **Aggression**
   Fundamentalists' greatest fear is difference – differences in ways of life and in views of life. They perceive diversity as aggressive, an attack on the ultimate truth that they believe they hold. Human life – others' and sometimes theirs – pale in comparison with the service of the truth.

4. **Sacrifice**
   Fundamentalists are so convinced of their ideals and principles that they are willing to make enormous sacrifices to realise them. Indeed, they need to engage in sacrifices as a demonstration of their commitment to their ideals and principles, and of their compliance with the leader's demands.

5. **Endurance**
   Fundamentalists value the ability to endure pain and suffering in the name of their intolerance of other attitudes or aspirations. It recommits them to the ideal of making sameness out of difference.

The Golden Rule Across the World's Religions: Thirteen Texts

Baha'i Faith

Lay not on any soul a load that you would not wish to be laid upon you, and desire not for anyone the things you would not desire for yourself.

Baha'u'llah, **Gleanings**

Buddhism

Treat not others in ways that you yourself would find hurtful.

The Buddha, **Udana – Varga 5.18**

Christianity

In everything, do to others as you would have them do to you; for this is the law and the prophets.

Jesus, **Matthew 7:12**

Confucianism

One word sums up the basis of all good conduct... loving-kindness. Do not do to others what you do not want done to yourself.

Confucius, **Analects 15.23**

Hinduism

This is the sum of duty: do not do to others what would cause pain if done to you.

Mahabharata 5:1517

Islam

Not one of you truly believes until you wish for others what you wish for yourself.

The Prophet Muhammad, **Hadith**

Jainism

One should treat all creatures in the world as one would like to be treated.

Mahavira, **Sutrakritanga 1.11.33**

Judaism

What is hateful to you, do not do to your neighbour. This is the whole Torah; all the rest is commentary. Go and learn it.

Hillel, **Talmud, Shabbath 31a**

Native Spirituality

We are as much alive as we keep the earth alive.

Chief Dan George

Sikhism

I am a stranger to no one; and no one is a stranger to me.

Indeed, I am a friend to all.

Guru Granth Sahib, p.1299

Taoism

Regard your neighbour's gain as your own gain and your neighbour's loss as your own loss.

Lao Tzu, **T'ai Shang Kan Ying P'ien, 213-218**

Unitarianism

We affirm and promote respect for the interdependent web of all existence of which we are a part.

Unitarian principle

Zoroastrianism

Do not do unto others whatever is injurious to yourself.

Shayast-na-Shayast 13.29

This poster contains the thirteen texts that appear on page 22.

Described as a 'movie', a slide presentation – related to the poster – was created by Ryan Nutter, aged 17. For each of the 13 traditions, the 'Golden Rule' quotation is given, with the tradition's symbol, a summary of its main beliefs and practices, and music or chanting, characteristic of the tradition.

Dialogue

The Dialogue Decalogue (below) is derived from ideas in the article by Leonard Swidler, 'Ground Rules for Inter-religious, Inter-cultural Dialogue'

THE DIALOGUE DECALOGUE

1. **Learning, changing and growing**
   The purpose of dialogue is to understand reality better and to act on that enhanced understanding – not to force change on others, as happens in debate.

2. **Two-sidedness**
   Dialogue is between two partners or groups of partners. It needs to take place both within and between communities.

3. **Honesty, sincerity and trust**
   Each partner needs to be willing to reveal any difficulties they have with their own tradition and assume that the other will do the same. Where there is no trust, there is no dialogue.

4. **Comparisons**
   Those engaged in dialogue should not compare their ideals with their partner's practice but rather their ideals with their partner's ideals and their practice with their partner's practice.

5. **Self-definition and dynamism**
   Each partner should define themselves, that is, crystallise and convey what it means to them to be a member of their religious tradition, from the inside. Others can only describe what it looks like from the outside. Because dialogue is dynamic, it can deepen, expand and modify self-definition.

6. **Open-mindedness and integrity**
   Partners should not make assumptions about points of disagreement that might emerge. Rather, they should listen to each other openly and be willing to agree with one another, while maintaining integrity with their own tradition.

7. **Equality**
   Dialogue can take place only between equals. If only one partner is teaching about their tradition and the other partner is only learning about another tradition, or if one partner thinks the other is inferior, it is not true dialogue.

8. **From the known to the unknown**
   Dialogue works best if it starts on common ground, creates trust and moves to more thorny issues later on.

9. **Self-criticism**
   Dialogue partners need to be critical of themselves and their own tradition. If a partner feels that they or their tradition has all the answers, dialogue is not simply unnecessary but actually impossible.

10. **From within**
    A religion or ideology is not merely in the head but also in the heart. It is not only individual but also communal. Those in dialogue should try to understand their partner's religion or ideology 'from within' – almost as if they were a part of it.

The Dialogue Decalogue can be a valid launch-pad for discussions – between teachers or between pupils – about ways in which classroom talk can become dialogue.

A teacher education session or a lesson for older pupils might involve comparing The Dialogue Decalogue (page 23) with the Five Features of Fundamentalism (page 21). These starter questions might be helpful:

■ Why does a fundamentalist not engage in dialogue?

■ Conversely, why would those who engage in dialogue not be fundamentalist?

■ Are there are similarities between fundamentalism (as outlined in the Five Features of Fundamentalism) and dialogue (as outlined in The Dialogue Decalogue)?

Engage teachers or older pupils in revisiting 'What we call Islam is a mirror in which we see ourselves' (page 13):

■ How does the schedule of attitudes to Islam that are explained there relate to the principles in 'The Dialogue Decalogue'?

■ Create a schedule of attitudes to another religion, ideology or philosophical life-stance: it may not be feasible to discover six separate points; the values of this activity are in empathy and reflective distance.

To conclude...

The twelve quotations – from a range of sources – on page 25 focus on the themes in the C-R-E-A-D structure. They have varied possible applications, including some of the strategies that appear in Part III. Formed into cards, for example, they might be used – in teacher education sessions or for pupils' learning activities – for matching, ranking and sorting.

Stand for SOMETHING
or you'll fall for ANYTHING.
graffiti on a bridge

One man's religion is
another man's belly laugh.
Robert Heinlein

Reality leaves a lot
to the imagination.
John Lennon

On l'interdit d'interdire.
(It is forbidden to forbid.)
French student slogan, 1968

We send missionaries to China so the
Chinese can get to heaven but we won't
let them into our country.
Pearl S. Buck

Do not take care of your own body and
another person's soul. Rather take care of
your own soul and another
person's body.
Rabbi Mendel of Kotsk

I do not want my house to be walled in
on all sides and my windows stifled. I
want all cultures of all lands to blow
about my house as freely as possible.
But I refuse to be blown off my
feet by any.
Mohandas K. Gandhi

One must verify or expel his doubts and
convert them into the certainty of
YES or NO.
Thomas Carlyle

I have sometimes yielded to the
temptation, when challenged that my
views are ambiguous, to declare that it is
better to be vaguely right than
definitely wrong.
*Rabbi Louis Jacobs (1920-2006), We Have
Reason To Believe (4th edition)*

The well educated have been taught to
believe that they can know nothing and
that they can draw no independent
conclusions about truth, unless they cite
study and 'experts' have affirmed it.
'Studies show' is to the modern secular
college graduate what 'Scripture says' is
to the religious fundamentalist.
Dennis Prager, talk show host

Having a clear faith, based on the creed
of the church, is often labelled today as a
fundamentalism... Whereas relativism,
which is letting oneself be tossed and
'swept along by every wind of teaching',
looks like the only attitude acceptable to
today's standards.
Pope Benedict XVI, 2005

The idea of the sacred is quite simply
one of the most conservative notions in
any culture, because it seeks to turn
other ideas – uncertainty, progress,
change – into crimes.
*Salman Rushdie, 'Is Nothing Sacred?'
Herbert Reade Memorial Lecture,
6 February 1990*

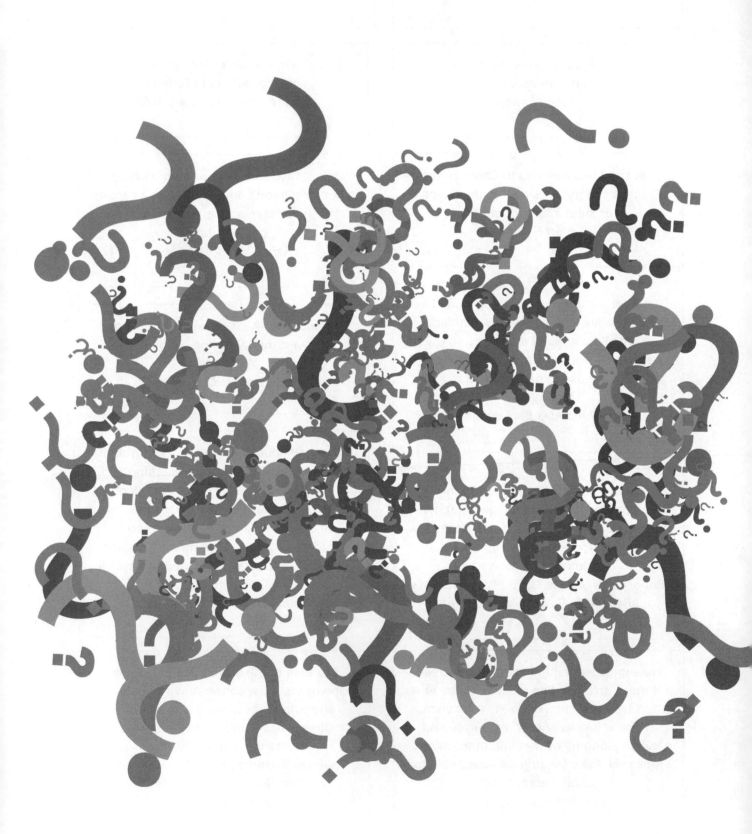

PART II
CHARTING A COURSE
guidance on approaching the issues in schools

☐ The Escape

☐ Talking, Teaching and Taboos

☐ Questions, Questions, Questions

☐ Decisions, Decisions, Decisions

☐ Planning and Preparing

☐ The Return

■ The Escape

She'd done all the marking, sorted out materials for the morning and was tidying her desk, ready to head for home. Before she left, something told her to cross the room and look in on Houdini. He was lying flat and motionless on the floor of his cage. She tapped the roof but he didn't hear. She opened the wire door and gingerly touched his body with the back of her finger. He didn't move but was not yet cold.

The children would be heartbroken. They all loved Houdini, named for his adventurous nature and his daring escapes. Staying in at break and playing with Houdini was a reward for any child who'd made a special effort. She'd had to draw up a rota of feeders and cage-cleaners, to stop the squabbles.

She was gripped with worry and fear, and she had to act fast. A plastic bag came hastily to hand, and Houdini was wrapped and popped in the bin. The cleaners would empty it later. It was not yet five. If she hurried, she could make it to the pet shop before it closed.

Luckily there were hamsters in stock and she bought the one that most resembled Houdini. When the children arrived the next morning, the cage was back in its place, complete with hamster.

'What's happened to Houdini?' was the immediate cry. 'His fur's a funny colour!'

A curious crowd gathered around the cage. 'And he's gone thin in the night!'

'That's not Houdini. Houdini doesn't get frightened and hide.'

'Where's Houdini gone, Miss?'

Try as she might, she was utterly unable to convince the class that the hamster in the cage was their Houdini, that he was all right and that they might have forgotten what he looked like or how he behaved. In the end, she pulled rank and literacy beckoned.

But she knew she was in deep trouble. The children were unsettled all day and kept asking about Houdini. Some were in tears. They knew he wasn't there and they needed to know why. Some seemed sad, some seemed frightened and some seemed confused.

Somehow the day passed. When the children had gone, she finally faced herself and what had happened – and what she had done about what happened. She called for help.

■ Talking, teaching and taboos

We might be tempted to judge this teacher. It's wrong to lie, arguably even worse to lie to our pupils. It was also pointless to try and fool them, as they'd be bound to know – a case of low expectations in the extreme. She hadn't protected them from sadness, fear or confusion: they were sad, frightened and confused, anyway. Even if she never owned up, the children would surely know she'd been pretending and lying, so how could she expect them to trust her and take her seriously again? She'd lost her moral authority and made the whole thing worse. Perhaps most of all, she had deprived the children of the experience of burying Houdini and grieving for him. Her actions begged the question: what do we tell the children?

We might be tempted to understand and identify with this teacher. It was the children's grief that she couldn't cope with and that's why she tried to escape. When she called for help, she explained that she has trouble with death: she couldn't face telling the children and having a funeral, involving them in creating the ritual and composing eulogies. She hadn't wanted to upset them, she said. She just wanted them to be happy.

Many of us do that, though in a less dramatic or extreme way. As teachers, there are some things that we find it difficult to talk about, for personal or professional reasons, and there are questions we dodge. It might be because they're taboos in our society. There might be administrative or curricular pressures at the time. Whatever the reason, we avoid speaking about them – and then they become unspeakable.

Children and young people need to know that they can express their sorrow, anxiety, anger or fear, whether their feelings derive from a tragedy at school or a terror attack that's in the news. They need us to create a safe climate for doing this. There is no more convincing way for us to give permission for their authenticity than through our own willingness, on occasions, to express such emotions ourselves. We may

imagine that it will make us seem weak but we are likely to seem – and to be – stronger. There are times when we have to be big enough to be small.

There is a thin line, of course, between being emotionally transparent and indulging ourselves or living out our lives in our classrooms. Our professionalism lies in spotting this line and never over-stepping it.

Part of the problem in Houdini's class was that there was no history of relating to matters of pain: no shared experience, for example, of reading stories about death or of talking about loss. For all the reading and writing that provided the escape hatch on the morning after Houdini's death, there was no practice in what we have come to call emotional literacy.

Part of the solution, then, is to create a culture of dealing with sensitive issues before they arise, before a hamster dies or a bomb detonates; that is, not wait for the crisis or even anticipate it but, rather, be proactive.

■ Questions, questions, questions

- ■ Will I get blown up?
- ■ Is my family all right while I'm at school?
- ■ Why are people hateful and violent?
- ■ Is it wrong to get back at them?
- ■ Why do some people want to kill themselves?
- ■ What has something happening in another country got to do with me?
- ■ Are some religions better than others?
- ■ Why does God let bad things happen?
- ■ How can we go on?
- ■ Who cares?

These are just some of the painful and searching questions that children and young people ask when tragedy strikes. Questions about personal safety, about human nature, about ethical responses, about the scope of our mental world, about the purpose of religion, about clinging to love, about recovering hope ...

We know that such questions may be blurted out, apparently out of the blue, or we may be taken aside to hear a whispered anguish. We also know that such questions may not find expression in words at all but manifest themselves in behaviour and body language, in attitude and mood. They are better out than in, and our skills may be tested in enabling children and young people to give their questions voice.

Sometimes a person's questions can be stimulated by responding to the questions of someone else, and literature and the arts are powerful vehicles in this search. Some of the stories and images in Part III have been included with this need in mind, along with the need to reflect on tragic events.

■ Decisions, decisions, decisions

A professional tennis player makes thousands of decisions in the course of a championship: whether to use backhand... stay back... head for the other side of the court... go for a passing shot or a drop shot... and so on – and each with split second timing.

So do we teachers – hundreds in a single lesson. Our significant but relatively relaxed decisions at the planning stage utterly pale in comparison with the number, speed and complexity of the on-the-hoof decisions we make in the classroom; and, like the tennis player, we are sometimes wrong-footed! Our decisions are even more complicated because our strategy is more involved. For the tennis player, there is one objective: to win. For us teachers, success is more complex, variegated and layered, and there are several kinds of success, including some that do not become apparent for years.

SENSITIVITY AND CONTROVERSY: WORKING DEFINITIONS

■ Sensitivity may be understood as referring to matters that invoke intense or delicate emotions, including those around bodily functions, personal intimacy and family loss. For example, the children were sensitive to the disappearance of Houdini; the teacher was sensitive to the death of Houdini. Other people who are not directly involved may be sympathetic or empathetic. Even if they are not, they are unlikely to take issue with the sensitivity shown.

■ Controversy may be understood as referring to matters about which there is more than one point of view and where unanimity is, by definition, impossible. For example, the teacher's handling of the death of Houdini is controversial. Frequently, people who are not directly involved in a situation have views about it if they feel that it affects them indirectly or if there are ethical principles at stake.

■ Sometimes a situation involves both sensitivity and controversy. For example, after the London bombings children and young people at school expressed feelings of fear, sorrow, anxiety and hatred: a matter of sensitivity. They also had a range of views about why these events had happened and what action should be taken to prevent further bombings: a matter of controversy. The sensitive and controversial responses were inevitably intertwined and mutually reinforcing.

As teachers, we need to think on the spot about, among other things, whether to:

■ ignore a pupil's irritating behaviour in the hope that it will dissipate

■ smile – and risk appearing less than serious

■ express anger or dismay in words or gesture or both – or not at all

■ interfere in a dispute between pupils or let them sort it out

■ intervene in a discussion or let it take its course

■ wade in and help a pupil who's floundering or leave them to struggle

■ ditch the lesson that was planned because it's not working

■ give an activity more time than planned because it's going so well

Most such decisions are based around aspects of control and involve a balancing act. Decisions in handling controversial issues paradoxically require both more control and less. When dealing with conflict, confusion and complexity, we recall, pupils need to live with paradox; here we as teachers also need to live with paradox.

Navigating the sensitive or the controversial – and especially the sensitive-and-controversial – is the most demanding of all our tasks as teachers. It is a task that is loaded with tensions, in every sense of the word. In an open and pluralist society and in a school that is committed to openness and pluralism, there are enormous challenges to – and conflicts within – our personal and professional sense of integrity as we support the process of discovery. The F-I-N-D checklist of separate but related questions for reflection can be supportive in clarifying our approach:

THE F-I-N-D APPROACH TO DISCOVERY OF SELF AND OTHERS

F Freedom of speech, freedom from fear

■ Is there a climate of respect and trust? Have we established ground rules for how we handle evidence and relate to one another?

■ Do all the pupils feel free to speak their minds? Do I need to encourage them?

■ Are some pupils intimidating in their speech or behaviour? Do I need to discourage them? Are there ideas that should not be voiced?

I Inwardly, outwardly, upwardly

■ Is there a spirit of inward reflection – or are people just peddling stereotypes and stock phrases?

■ Is the sharing open, outward and authentic? Does what is said match what is thought and felt?

■ Amid the sorrow, anger, hatred and fear, is there a sense of something beautiful that might emerge – a reason to hope, an upward glance?

N Neutrality

■ Regardless of what I think and feel – and how much the controversy affects me personally – am I being procedurally neutral?

■ Am I doing everything I can to ensure balance and fairness in the topics I focus on and the materials I choose or create?

■ Does my bias and prejudice affect the way I relate to individuals or groups of pupils? Have I bracketed myself out?

D Disagreeing without being disagreeable

■ Have the pupils grasped the idea that the medium is the message?

■ Have they learned to discuss and debate in a mood of sweet reasonableness?

■ Do they appreciate that people are complex rather than caricatures or cardboard characters? Can they see the person to be accepted behind the ideas to be rejected?

■ Planning and preparing

A set of decisions also apply to teaching and learning in situations where the subject matter is not prompted by an experience involving an individual or group in the class or a high profile event in the local, national or international news. When nothing is happening, as it were, there are additional challenges of selecting and presenting material to stimulate personal thought, the clarification of values, the enhancement of relationships and responsible social action.

The chart on page 32 delineates three possible approaches that RE (and sometimes related areas of the curriculum) can take towards religious, cultural and ideological diversity. The approach described as Pluralism (third column) forms the basis for the teaching strategies and learning resources that appear in Part III. These strategies and resources will be most effective in the hands of those who are committed to pluralism in their teaching about religions, ideologies and cultures.

Part III is not a scheme of work but rather a bank of materials or an a la carte menu, from which you can choose – within the framework of the National Curriculum or the local Agreed Syllabus – so as to meet your pupils' needs.

■ The Return

As luck would have it, the bin had not been emptied the previous day and the teacher retrieved Houdini's body. That was the easy part. The hard part was facing the children.

She started the day by reading *Badger's Parting Gifts*, with the children on the carpet, and then led a discussion on the ways in which the animals in the story memorialised their beloved Badger. It reminded the children of Houdini. She knew that they knew.

She cleared her throat. 'Sometimes grownups get frightened, not just children. People do silly things when they're afraid. Houdini died. It made me sad and I was scared it would make you sad as well. I didn't want to tell you yesterday.'

There was a catch in her voice and her eyes were moist. A child crouched beside her and laid a comforting little hand on her shoulder.

They all talked about whether they should look at Houdini or touch him, and what they should do. Some children made a shroud, others a coffin. Some chose a spot in the school grounds and dug a grave. Yet others composed a eulogy.

Two children – the youngest and the oldest in the class – acted as pallbearers and the procession moved deliberately from the classroom to the graveside.

The children read their words, recalling their happiest memories of Houdini and extolling his highest virtues. The recorder group played its finest.

The teacher cried.

THE RESPONSE OF RELIGIOUS EDUCATION
TO RELIGIOUS, CULTURAL AND IDEOLOGICAL DIVERSITY

	Assimilation	Separatism	Pluralism
Ideology	Total absorption of minority group into mainstream	Encapsulation of minority culture; withdrawal of minority groups; self-help and separate provision	Minority groups' participation in a just society; equal rights with majority; cultural status for all
Emphasis	On the majority	On minorities	On the majority and minority; currently only an ideal
Attitude to religion	Deficit hypothesis: 'true' religion v. 'false' religion	Avoidance of conflict: religion a private matter for individuals and minority communities	Interactional approach: religious variability; diversity celebrated; mutual enrichment; notion of religion in evolution
Approaches to religious education	Neo-confessional on the part of the majority	Confessional, on the part of the minority	Phenomenological
Curriculum content	Fossilised curriculum; high culture; narrowly ethnocentric	Ethnic studies; traditional scriptures	Curriculum permeated by openness to all cultural/religious sources. Awareness of stereotyping and religious prejudice.
Organisation of religious education	Christian ideas permeate many school subjects (especially literature, history); evangelism as a process of socialisation	Supplementary education: Qur'an schools (Muslim), heder (Jewish) etc.; religious maintenance for minorities in state schools	Mixed affiliation classrooms (all faiths and none); specialist Religious Studies teacher

PART III
CRAFT AND CURRICULUM
activities and resources

☐ Images for imagining

☐ Telling tales

☐ Plays and puzzles

☐ Reporting on reporting

■ Images for imagining

The use of optical illusions is one of the most effective ways of enabling pupils to perceive and appreciate that there are differing viewpoints – and that each can be valid. Visual perception games provide a valuable starting-point for an exploration of issues surrounding pluralism. In particular, they:

■ help to develop pupils' visual literacy, including their powers of observation and interpretation

■ encourage the habit of *not* jumping to conclusions

■ offer an experience of handling cognitive dissonance

■ provide opportunities for pupils to verbalise the non-verbal

■ are relevant to all age groups

■ can be used in a variety of curriculum contexts or free-standing

■ are fun!

Using the visuals

The 18 images on pages 37-47 are numbered for reference. Some are well known – although their origin may not be – and are presented here so that you can readily lay your hands on them. Others are much more unusual.

Note that although the approach to using optical illusions can be effective for all age groups, some specific images are more attractive to younger pupils (for example, 1, 2, 3, 7 and 9) while others require a sophistication that makes them more readily accessible to older pupils (for example, 5 and 6). A certain knowledge base of maps and mapping is needed to appreciate 14-17.

Once the developmentally appropriate visuals have been identified, they can be made into cards – with the page numbers omitted but the number of the visual retained – cut to size and, budget permitting, laminated: there are many and differing contexts in which these images can be used so this is likely to be a good investment of time and material.

The visuals are resources for a one-off or a series of focused lessons. However, they are most effective if used for a short part of a lesson, but repeatedly over a period. Establishing a mental framework that is open to diversity and to paradox cannot be ticked off as 'taught': it needs learning and unlearning and relearning, through a process of continual revisiting. By the way, this need makes this set of resources very useful to have handy for those spare minutes when a particular unit has been completed but there is no time – or it is inappropriate – to start a new unit; likewise, when a particular group has finished a task ahead of the rest of the class.

Finally, the proof of the pudding is in the pupils creating their own optical illusions, visual games or alternatives to the conventional presentations of reality. This might be accomplished through drawings by hand, computer-assisted graphics or collage.

A key to the angles taken in the visuals

- Some visuals are two-in-one in that they reveal different pictures according to which way they are turned. This applies to 1, 2, 3, 7, 9 and 10.

- In some visuals, there is more than one image, according to the way in which it is perceived – that is, which elements of the visual are focused on as dominant and which as dependent. This applies to 4, 5, 6, 12 and 13.

- In visual 11, additional images are incongruously embedded in an otherwise familiar and straightforward picture.

- In visual 8, the central image is 'lost' in the background.

- Images 14-18 are not optical illusions. They are presentations of the world in ways that challenge conventional views. Further detail appears below.

Information about and interpretation of the visuals

These visuals are ordered on an incline of difficulty or complexity, the ones appearing earliest being suitable for pupils across the age and attainment range, including young pupils.

1
- One way up: a smiling face
- The other way up: a frowning face

2
- One way up: the face of a young child with curly hair
- The other way up: the face of a bearded bald man

3
- One way up: a rabbit popping out of a top hat
- The other way up: a person wearing a top hat – with tufts of hair showing – and a pointed collar

4
- One reading: a white vase against a black background
- Another reading: two profiles – facing each other – silhouetted against a white background

5
- One reading: the left profile of a person with short, dark and slightly spiky hair
- Another reading: the three-quarter back view of a person wearing a coat and hood, approaching the entrance of a cave or igloo

6
- One reading: large three-quarter front profile of an apparently old woman with a large nose and pointed chin, looking downwards, and wearing an open jacket and loose headscarf, with a mop of curly hair on her forehead
- Another reading: small three-quarter back profile of an apparently young woman, with a choker necklace on her slender neck and a feathery headdress

7 ▨▨▨▨▨▨▨▨▨▨
- Tilted left: a duck
- Tilted right: a rabbit, sitting on its haunches

8 ▨▨▨▨▨▨▨▨
- Three-quarters back view of a black-spotted white dog, sniffing the ground, which is similarly spotted

9 ▨▨▨▨▨▨▨▨▨
- One way up: a young woman with thick wavy hair framing her face and a coronet on her head
- The other way up: an old woman with thick wavy hair drawn up on her head, a furrowed brow and protruding nose, and pointed edges round the neck of her blouse

10 ▨▨▨▨▨▨▨▨▨▨
- One way up: on a clump of grass, a large bird, clenching a frightened person in its beak; with a flock of birds flying low in the distance on the left
- The other way up: a large fish that has collided with a frightened person in a canoe, next to a islet that has sand and grass; with waves in the distance on the right

11 ▨▨▨▨▨▨▨▨
- The Mona Lisa with a tabby cat on her chest and a rabbit for a hand

12 ▨▨▨▨▨▨▨▨▨
- One reading: Don Quijote de la Mancha and Sancho Panza, with a windmill behind them (at which they might have tilted!), and the demons they were fighting in shadows all around
- Another reading: an old man, with very bushy eyebrows, and a wrinkled, bald pate but wild white hair at the back of his head

13 ▨▨▨▨▨▨▨▨▨
- One reading: a man and a woman (holding a baby) underneath an arch; with a dog lying on the cobblestone street
- Another reading: the left profile of a balding, white-haired man, with his right hand on his chest

14 ▨▨▨▨▨▨▨▨▨▨
- A so-called upside down map where north is at the bottom and south at the top. Given that 'top' and 'bottom' are not neutral descriptors, there has been a movement in the Antipodes to generate world maps such as this, sometimes with the slogan 'What's up, down under?' It challenges notions of up-ness and down-ness in map-making and this has implications for other contexts in which language and imagery are used in loaded ways.
- In McAthur's Univeral Correction Map, created in 1979, is a south-up map that positions Australia in the centre at the top.
- Other examples of maps that defy convention can be seen at www.flourish.org/upsidedownmap
- Comparisons of Mercator-based maps and the Peters projection – with their differing presentations of relative land sizes – are relevant here.
- For teachers and older pupils seeking to explore further ways in which maps can distort rather than present reality, *Seeing Through Maps: Many Ways to See the World*, by Denis Wood, Ward L. Kaiser and Bob Abramms may be helpful. It examines ways in which map projections reveal the perceptions of the world held by the mapmakers and it uncovers some of their hidden yet provocative messages. It argues that maps are propositions and can be used as tools of persuasion or exploitation.

15 ▨▨▨▨▨▨▨▨▨
- Heinrich Bünting's Clover Leaf Map (1581), one of his allegorical maps which he described as 'The whole world in a clover leaf, which is the crest of the city of Hanover, my beloved fatherland'.
- This and other medieval metaphorical representations of the planet can be seen at www.themaphouse.com
- The three continents of the 'Old World' are shown well-divided by the seas. Asia, Europe and Africa are in the form of three

cloverleaves centred on a vignette of the city of Jerusalem. The blue ocean is titled 'The Great Mediterranean Sea of the World'. Only the Red Sea (more accurately the Reed Sea or Sea of Reeds) is coloured red and shown separately. Parts of Scandinavia and America are shown at the extreme edges of the map. On the engraved seas there is a galleon afloat, sea monsters and an almost circular island named England.

■ There are features of up-ness in the position of Hanover.

■ This map was designed more for religious edification in Christian Europe than for geographical information. That which is not central but peripheral and that which is not connected but floating is of low value. The role of Jerusalem – both as centre and as connection – is palpable.

16

■ Entitled 'Mecca is in our heart', this map appears at www.qiblacentral.com, which states that it is a 'mathematically accurate projection'.

■ It is ingenious as a metaphor for the deep affection in which devout Muslims hold Makkah.

Images 15 and 16 are a thought-provoking pair for pupils to compare and contrast. It is preferable to use the two visuals side by side. This removes the up-ness and down-ness factors. As with all the images, creating single-image cards gives pupils greater scope in their application and enables them to manipulate the images more flexibly.

17

■ This world map places Mecca – or preferably 'Makkah' – at the centre of the planet Earth.

■ While it is may be the case that a map can be drawn to 'place' anywhere on the planet at the centre, there is a view amongst Islamic theologians and certainly mystics that the unique spirituality of Makkah makes it the true hub of the world wheel. The arguments are articulated and illustrated at www.qiblacentral.com: they are highly complicated – for all but the geography specialist – and therefore difficult to accept or reject in strictly cartographic terms. For this reason, pupils handling this and similar maps should be discouraged from viewing Makkah as the centre of the globe in a literal sense.

■ The use of 'world' as metaphor is as clear and powerful as its use to describe a physical space. It is therefore possible to interpret such a visual statement about the core of faith and of the key role that Makkah – and all that it means in Islam – plays in Muslim lives.

18

■ 'Moon Landscape' was one of several drawings by Petr Ginz, a 14-year-old Jewish boy, during his detention in Theresienstadt (Terezin), in 1942. He loved the natural world, was interested in astronomy and wanted to be a scientist when he grew up. The Nazis murdered him at Auschwitz in 1944.

■ Some of his work survived and is now at Yad V'Shem, the Holocaust Memorial Museum in Jerusalem.

■ On 16 January 2003, Israel's first astronaut, Colonel Ilan Ramon, was launched into space on the shuttle Columbia, whose mission tragically failed. All the astronauts had taken on board the spacecraft items of cultural significance: 'Moon Landscape' was among the items chosen by Colonel Ilan Ramon.

■ In 'Moon Landscape', the moon and the earth are reversed. Petr Ginz sees the earth from the perspective of the moon, but as the moon seems from earth-mystical, peaceful and full of light.

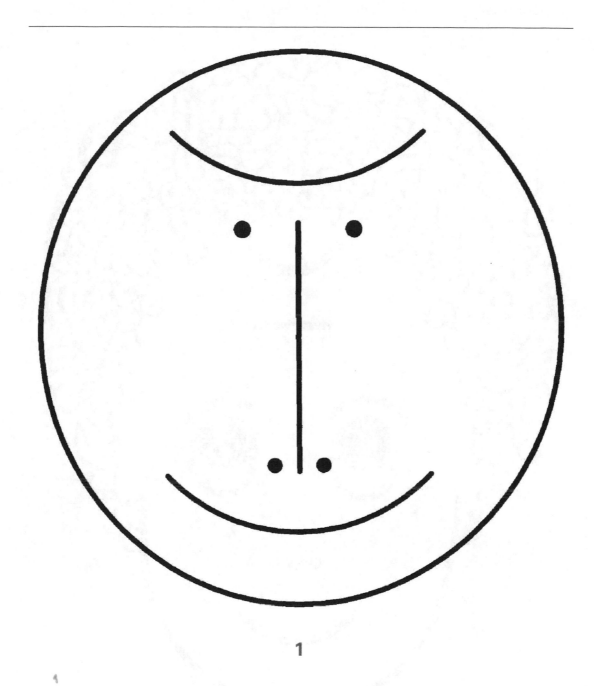

1

2

3

4

5

6

7

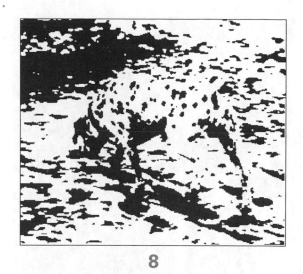

8

9

10

11

12

13

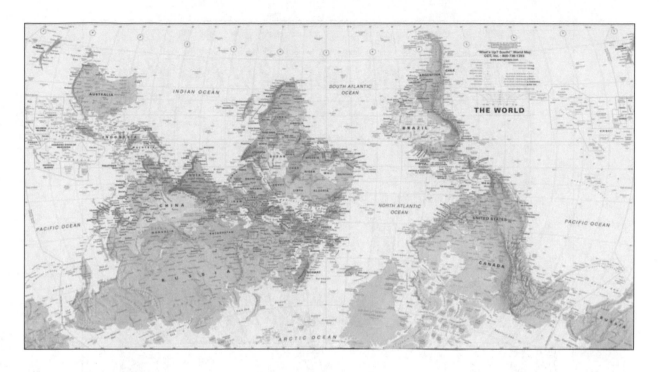

14

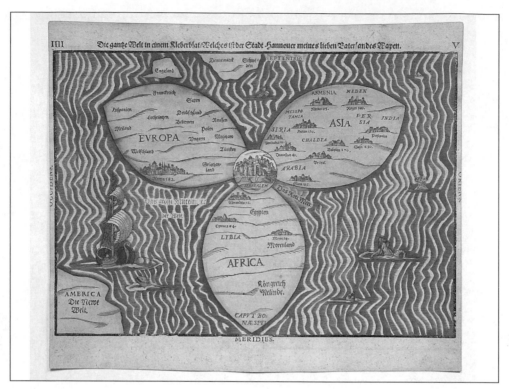

15

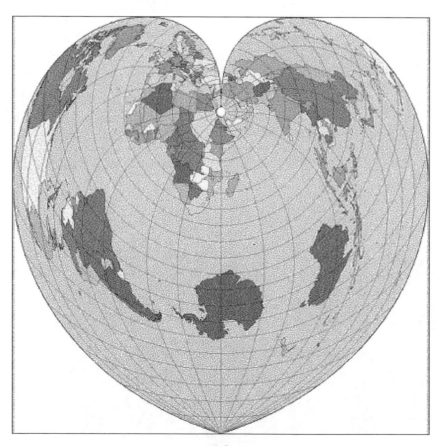

16

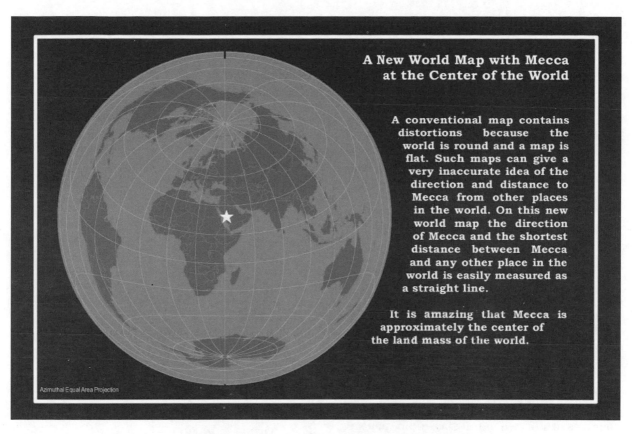

A New World Map with Mecca at the Center of the World

A conventional map contains distortions because the world is round and a map is flat. Such maps can give a very inaccurate idea of the direction and distance to Mecca from other places in the world. On this new world map the direction of Mecca and the shortest distance between Mecca and any other place in the world is easily measured as a straight line.

It is amazing that Mecca is approximately the center of the land mass of the world.

Azimuthal Equal Area Projection

17

18

■ Telling tales

For the purpose of using stories with pupils, the term 'story' can be taken to include:

■ quotations from scripture and other literature

■ re-tellings of traditional stories from scripture or folklore

■ contemporary stories with meaning, written or told

■ descriptions of religious rituals

■ accounts of historical or cultural events

■ anecdotes and snippets of biographies

■ sequences of photos or other images

Not all of us can be dramatic and accomplished storytellers and we don't all have to be – though we're probably better at it than we imagine. After all, we spend a lot of our lives telling stories about one thing or another. All the same, we may be nervous about acting as storyteller in the classroom, and we may find it difficult to juggle the roles of storyteller and classroom manager! We can't assume that pupils will automatically be attentive and responsive: there might be all kinds of distractions and unpredictable happenings.

Twelve strategies

It's very useful to have a range of educational strategies that help pupils engage with the story and its meaning – both in context and for themselves. These can be used for the fifteen stories on pages 55-77, as well as others of the kinds listed above. For each story, at least one – and usually several – of the twelve strategies can be used.

These twelve strategies are all quite simple exercises or activities that help pupils attend to a story and to explore its meaning, without having to intellectualise – at least at first. Some activities are better suited to some stories than others but, for any given story, there are likely to be several relevant activities. The twelve activities below begin with the simplest and shortest and end with the more complex and demanding. 'Story' is used to apply to the kinds of material listed above. Each activity is outlined under three headings.

What
A brief description of what the activity entails

How
Suggestions about classroom organisation, directions for pupils and any necessary preparations for the activity

Why
Some possible learning outcomes of the activity

1. Factual quizzes

What
■ Giving a test or quiz about factual details in a story that has been told or read.

How
■ *Either* prepare a set of questions in advance and present these to the pupils either before or after the story is told or read.

■ *Or* after the pupils have heard the story, ask them to construct a quiz and 'give' it to a partner or group.

☐ It may be useful to tell or read a story twice, with the second presentation coming after the quiz, and allow pupils to adjust their previous answers or fill in gaps.

Why
■ Pupils have to listen particularly carefully.

■ Pupils find it satisfying to memorise small details and answer questions correctly.

■ It helps pupils distinguish between essential and irrelevant details.

2. Cloze procedure

What
■ Blotting out certain words in a piece of text and getting pupils to decide how the gaps ought to be filled.

How
■ *Either* blot out certain particularly significant words, essential for understanding a story's meaning *or* blot out every nth word, regardless of how important it is.

■ You can present the story, with its gaps, to the whole class either by reading it aloud or by writing it on the board, a flip chart or overhead projector; or you can give it to the 'leader' of a small group who reads it slowly to the rest of the group; or it can be worked on by each pupil alone, followed by class or small group discussion, comparing and contrasting various suggestions.

■ Whichever method you use, it's a good idea to get pupils to think of more than one separate possibility for each gap, so that they have to reason and choose.

Why

■ Pupils have to attend closely to the sequence of events in a story and the characteristics of the language.

■ Pupils have to draw on the full range of their own language resources, and may well extend their active or passive vocabulary, thus acquiring specialist terms.

■ Pupils develop self-confidence from knowing that there is seldom a single 'correct' answer, and from seeing that their own suggestions are sometimes preferable to the words used in the original.

■ Pupils find the exercise both simple and challenging.

3. Sequencing

What

■ Cutting up a text – or a series of pictures – and getting pupils to piece it together again.

How

■ It's better to divide the class into groups: each member of a group holds one of the pieces of the text, and reads it aloud, in turn, to the others.

■ It's also possible to work with the whole class: have the text on large pieces of poster paper around the room, or on overhead projector.

Why

■ If it's carried out in small groups, pupils listen to each other closely, collaborate on the task, respecting each other, and develop self-respect – because everyone holds an indispensable resource!

■ Pupils develop self-confidence, through having a sense of being in charge of the material.

■ Pupils think about cause and effect, and therefore develop skills of speculation, reasoning and justifying.

■ Pupils become aware of the language styles used in scripture, folk tales and other stories.

■ Pupils come to see that there may be more than one 'right' answer.

4. Key Words

What

■ Getting pupils to join in the recitation of an important brief passage from a story, a poem or an extract from scripture or liturgy.

How

■ Choose a fairly brief passage from a story or a few lines or poetry or liturgy. The passage should preferably be in heightened language. It's often a good idea to ask the pupils to close their eyes during the readings.

■ Read the passage slowly to the class four times, as follows:

☐ Ask the pupils to listen as carefully as possible as you read the passage straight through.

☐ As you read to the pupils this time, ask them to pick out in their minds any words or phrases which they like or which mean something special to them. Ask them to let their thoughts settle on that word and roll it around in their mind.

☐ Ask pupils to say aloud the words or phrases they have chosen, at the same time that you say them.

☐ Ask the class to join in reciting the passage as fully as possible, speaking along with you. By this stage, they will almost certainly know the whole passage by heart.

Why

■ Pupils use and develop their listening skills.

■ Pupils note and appreciate heightened language, including the use of metaphor, repetition and cadence that are essential characteristics of liturgy, parable and other story forms.

5. Messages

What

■ Getting pupils to summarise a story's point or message with a slogan, phrase or proverbial saying.

How

■ Prepare in advance a set of slogans – the kind that appears on badges, T-shirts, coffee mugs or greetings cards, or proverbs. Ask the pupils choose from these, or adapt them, or use them as models for their own phrases.

■ Instead, you can get the pupils to invent their own messages from cold.

■ Either way, pupils have to summarise in a pithy and striking way what they understand to be the message or moral of the story, ritual or event.

■ It's useful for the pupils to distinguish between and discuss two main types of messages: those that only make sense to insiders; and those that mean something to anyone.

■ It's important that pupils should compare and contrast different suggestions for summarising the same story, choose between alternatives, and give their reasons.

Why

■ Pupils will probably find it easier to remember the story, ritual or event.

■ They are helped to explore and articulate the basic meaning of the story, ritual or event.

■ They use and develop their imagination, and their ability to express complex ideas through metaphor and allusion.

6. Interrupting

What

■ Breaking into the telling or reading of a story with a question or query.

How

■ It can be a whole class or small group activity, led either by you or by one or more of the pupils.

■ You might use questions like these:

☐ 'Imagine the scene now. What can you see, hear, smell and touch?'

☐ 'What do you think is going to happen next?'

☐ 'What do you think so-and-so in the story might be thinking or feeling now?'

☐ 'If you could enter the story and speak to the characters, what would you say?'

☐ 'Make up some other information about so-and-so, based on what you already know about them: what do they look like? what hobbies or interests do they have? how would they vote in an election? what might they say about such-and-such? what makes them laugh or cry?'

Why

■ Pupils enter more fully with their imagination into the story's events and this enables some of the issues that the story raises to emerge naturally.

■ They have to fantasise, guess, empathise and speculate.

■ They appreciate the role of significant people in religious stories.

7. Interrogating
What

■ Getting pupils to ask masses of questions about a story or part of a story.

How

■ If you want the pupils to work on their own, give each one a piece of text printed on a large sheet of paper, with plenty of space all around.

■ If you want the pupils to work in small groups, give each group a very large sheet, with a story or extract from a story pasted in the middle.

■ In the margins round the text, ask them to write as many short questions as possible – either factual or speculative.

■ Once they've written lots of questions, ask the pupils to speculate about some possible answers, and to identify (say, with a coloured marker) the questions they find most relevant to the meaning of the story or event.

■ A variation on, and extension of, this activity is to get pupils to pass their sheet to another individual or group and get them to respond to the questions that have been written there. It's a good idea for the pupils to use a different coloured pen so that questions and responses can be clearly identified.

Why

■ Pupils have to be imaginative and therefore become more receptive to the meaning of the story, ritual or event.

■ They are required to pay closer attention than might otherwise be the case.

■ They become self-confident when they feel they are in charge of the material rather than being merely passive recipients.

8. Re-telling and re-writing
What

■ Getting pupils to re-tell or re-write a story from a different point of view, in a different style, or in a different context.

How

There are several possibilities including:

■ pupils telling the story from the point of view of one of the characters: they can bring in their own feelings and perceptions and elaborate on events and experiences that are only touched on in the original.

■ pupils telling the story or part of the story in another form, for example, as a newspaper article, television script, letter, diary entry, minutes of a meeting.

■ pupils transposing the story to a different culture, or to a different period of history.

Why

■ Pupils have to identify and attend to the most important features in the story or event.

■ They may well develop new meanings and so can appreciate the living process of passing traditional stories on from one age to another, and from one culture to another.

9. PICTURING
What

■ Getting pupils to explore their responses to a story by choosing or making pictures.

How

■ Post some photographs or other pictures on the walls of the classroom or place them on some of the furniture. Or give each group a selection of small pictures, for example, postcards and magazine cutouts.

■ Read or tell the story to the class as a whole.

■ Ask the pupils, first on their own and then in pairs or groups, to choose the image or images which best express for them what the story was really about.

■ Instead, you can give the class piles of old magazines and ask them to create collages that illustrate what they felt the story was about.

Why

■ Pupils are likely to find it much easier to respond to a story non-verbally and non-cerebrally, at least to start with.

■ They can see that narrative accounts and other stories, like photographs and collages, involve selection, framing, perspective, juxtaposition, composition, and so on.

10. REALIA

What

■ Getting pupils to imagine and create small scraps of material to fill in a story's background.

How

■ The possibilities include: shopping lists; letters and notes of various kinds; notices; advertisements; news cuttings; extracts from a school report or record of achievement; drafts and jottings; diary extracts; a telegram; publicity leaflets; greetings cards; telephone messages; e-mails; Internet home pages.

■ You can then ask the pupils to make a collection of realia for a scrapbook or wall display.

Why

■ Pupils are encouraged to use wit, humour and imagination.

■ They are helped to remember the main outline of a story.

■ They may discover additional meanings for the story and appreciate the richness condensed in it.

11. FROZEN FRAMES

What

■ Asking pupils to imagine and represent a single scene from a story or a specific religious ritual or event, in order to illustrate the story as a whole.

How

■ *Either* ask pupils, in small groups or on their own, to describe a chosen scene in words or sketch it roughly.

■ *Or* ask them in small groups to sculpt their chosen scene, by creating a tableau; it may be valuable for you or a pupil to sketch or photograph the tableaux, to promote and focus further discussion. These might be used to create a photo album or collage, depicting stages in the life of a character in the story or a sequence of rites of passage in the life of a person in a particular religious tradition. Alternatively, one picture might be the 'book cover' of the story.

Why

■ Pupils have to choose and respond to what they feel is a particularly significant episode in a story.

■ Through the processes of visualising and sculpting, pupils may discover and create a story's deeper meanings.

■ They may discover ways of adapting or developing a story to new situations.

■ They are helped to remember a story as a whole by having to focus in great detail on one particular scene or episode.

12. GUIDED FANTASY

What

■ Getting the pupils to visualise the scenes and events in a story as vividly as possible in their mind's eye.

How

■ It might be useful to begin with a relaxation exercise to help pupils still their minds and be more able to concentrate on the story. Or ask pupils to focus on certain objects – either everyday classroom things or special artefacts – so that they can attend to their own sensations and feelings before attending to the story.

■ Ask the pupils to close their eyes. Read them the story quite slowly, with frequent pauses and possibly certain questions that might help them visualise the events and scenes.

■ At the end, it's very important to bring them back to the present very gently and give them opportunities to describe and reflect on what they 'saw'.

Why

■ Pupils use and develop their imaginations and capacities for empathy.

■ Pupils are likely to remember the story far more vividly.

■ Pupils are likely to find that the stories, rituals and events take on a life of its own.

Fifteen texts appear on pages 55-77. With two exceptions, they are traditional stories representing between them a range of cultures and spiritual or religious traditions. They have been recast in contemporary settings and in contemporary language, and some have been considerably amplified. The two exceptions are *A Match*, based on an urban myth, and the extract from the play *Nathan the Wise*.

Each text is followed by notes on its background and clusters of reflective questions that can be used to stimulate discussion or as a basis for other learning activities.

'Telling Tales At A Glance' on page 54 lists the fifteen texts, with a note about the tradition from which each comes, its major motifs and messages, and the approximate pupil age for which it is appropriate.

TELLING TALES AT A GLANCE

Title	Tradition	Main motifs and messages	Age-range	Page
All Together	Hindu	■ the whole being more than sum of its parts ■ the need for collaboration ■ illusions	7-13	55
Inside Out	Islamic	■ judgements and prejudice ■ inter-group hostility ■ life's surprises	7-13	56
Growing up	Christian	■ tasks and tests ■ talents ■ risk-taking	7-13	58
A Dream of a Place	Jewish	■ collaboration ■ the realisation of dreams ■ other-centredness	7-13	60
Taking sides	Sikh	■ empathy ■ generosity of spirit ■ persons and positions	7-13	61
Firing a shot	Buddhist	■ pointless questioning ■ the priority of setting priorities ■ the persistence of pain	7-13	62
Just a Drop	Jewish	■ seeking and finding ■ justice, prayer and repentance ■ impossible choices	7-13	64
What It's Worth	Islamic	■ desperation and desire ■ weighing things up ■ inner and outer wealth	7-13	66
Something in the Air	Hindu	■ the pervasive nature of evil ■ terror ■ saving forces	7-13	68
The Stonecutter	Tao	■ appearance and reality ■ aspirations and their realisation ■ the constancy of change	7-18	70
Cup Final	Christian	■ quests and questions ■ the worries of the world ■ elusive realities	10-13	71
Whoever Comes This Way	African	■ power struggles ■ the nature of winning ■ inner strength	10-18	73
A Match	Modern Western, unknown	■ the equality of human beings ■ the questionable rightness of war ■ the nature of God	10-17	74
Five Journeys	Buddhist	■ seeking the meaning of life ■ emergent needs and changes of course ■ missions accomplished	14-18	75
Nathan the Wise extract	Christian	■ trust and trustworthiness ■ interfaith dialogue ■ the impossibility of absolutes	14-18	76

All Together

A wedding was the last thing in the world on Ms Hind's mind. Everyone told her it was time she settled down, but she didn't fancy the idea at all. It wasn't the actual ceremony she minded. In fact, she liked being the centre of attention and she hadn't been to a decent party for ages. What really bothered her was the idea of being tied down and not being able to do what she wanted. She had her career to think of.

'If you met the right man,' her mother said softly, 'someone who'd make a fuss of you and let you have a bit of your own life, you wouldn't feel like that. Perhaps you could do things together. Your father and I only want you to be happy... There are so many really nice young men interested in you but you never give them a chance.'

'Oh, Mum, they're such creeps!'

'Not all of them, dear. Why don't you let us arrange something?'

'All right – but only if I can choose.'

'Of course, darling.'

Mr and Mrs. Hind worked really fast and lined up six eligible bachelors for her to meet. Their daughter had been working fast too and had devised a clever plan to find out which guy – if any – was the man for her. She got the idea from a party game she played when she was about ten: everyone is blindfolded and they have to guess what something is by feeling it.

Getting hold of an elephant for a day wasn't exactly easy but well worth the effort. She led it into the yard and gave it plenty to eat so it wouldn't be noisy and give the game away.

'Is this their idea of 'Mr Wonderful'?' Ms Hind thought when she saw her admirers. They all agreed to the test.

'Too tight?' she asked as she blindfolded the first one.

'It's fine, my sweet.'

'My sweet!' she thought. 'Yuk!' And she led him into the yard to identify the mystery object.

'I hope you're not peeping!' she said to the second one.

'You know I only have eyes for you!'

'Good grief!' she muttered. 'This way, please.'

'Ouch! you're hurting me!' screamed the third, but she tugged the wimp by the arm and led him into the yard with the others.

'What kind of knot are you using?' the fourth suitor enquired.

'A strong one!' retorted Ms Hind, thinking to herself, 'What a fool!'

The fifth in line stood with his arms by his side and let her apply the blindfold but she never respected anyone who seemed weak.

By the time it was the turn of the sixth, and tallest, there was no pleasing her at all.

The six rivals staggered about in the yard, their arms stretched out in front of them, and finally each one caught hold of one part of the elephant's body.

'Well, what is it?' Ms Hind called from the balcony.

The first one was holding the trunk. 'It's a pipe, my sweet!'

'Wrong – my sweet!' she snapped.

Nearby, the second called out, 'It's a spear!' He was gripping the animal's tusk.

'No!'

'I'm sure it's a tree,' the third chipped in. He had wrapped his arms round one of the legs.

'Nothing like!' she shouted. Three down – three to go!

From the tail end, the fourth in the guessing – game yelled, 'A rope!'

'Wrong as well!'

All this time, the fifth contestant had been stroking the huge creature's side.

'It's definitely a wall!'

'It's definitely not!'

Finally, the tall man had stretched to the elephant's ear.

'With this, my love, I shall fan you on hot days!'

'I'm cool already!' she rebuffed him.

'You have all missed the point. You can't break anything into bits and expect to know that it's really like. It isn't even all the bits added up. You have to see it as a whole. If you'd only talked to each other and shared what you knew, you could have worked it out. Nobody ever has all the answers and sometimes we think we see things that aren't even there. So, you're dying to know what it is? It is an elephant. Take off your blindfolds and see for yourself.'

But when they turned round to look... the elephant had vanished.

***

Background and treatment
This story probably once came from India though it has been told in many countries with slightly different details. It is a good example of the way stories change by being told over and over again.

Usually, the characters are *actually* blind and it is a king who gives them the puzzle to solve about how we see life. Quite a lot of Hindu folktales have parents looking for a suitable match for their daughter or son. This modern version combines the two kinds of stories but with a slight twist: the young woman wants to take her pick...

Reflective questions
■ What might have happened if the six young men had shared what they felt? Would they have worked out that it was an elephant? If they did, what would be Ms Hind's problem then? How could the story go on from there?

■ Why had the elephant vanished when they took off their blindfolds? Was it ever there at all? What could the elephant represent?

■ In what other situations is the whole more than the sum of its parts?

Inside Out
'He's gone! He's gone!' shrieked Fari, jumping up and down, her nose twitching in excitement.

'Sh! What if he hasn't...?' Imfar squeaked. But as they spoke, they saw through a crack in the wall the familiar shape of Simsim, the neighbourhood cat, their most determined persecutor. He was climbing into a taxi, while the driver strapped the luggage onto the roof rack and slammed the door. 'The airport, please!' the cat miaowed, adding with an air of importance, 'Saudi Arabian check-in! And please hurry! I simply *must* be on the flight to Jedda!'

The cab sped off down the road and the mice leapt for joy. 'When the cat's away, mice will play!' Asfar reminded them all. 'And are we going to play!' Edfar tooted her flute, Olfar beat his drum; they all joined hands in a circle and danced so fast that the mouse-hole itself started to rock. Soon Urfar appeared with plates of nibbles – crunchy nuts, dried fruit and ripe cheese. Their tiny feet were blistered from dancing and their jaws ached from laughing but they were contented little mice that flopped onto cushions and fell into a deep sleep.

By the time they woke up, Simsim was landing at Jedda. It had been a smooth, comfortable flight and already he had got to know some of his fellow pilgrims. It was the time of the year when Muslims from all over the world make this journey to the Ka'aba – the first altar to Allah – and the place where the Prophet Muhammad was born. It was near Makka that Allah had given the Prophet so many ideas for the world, so going there was getting in touch with all of that inside you.

Not every Muslim would be there this year but they all felt they should make the trip at least once in their life, if they could. For most of them, it would be a one-off and that was partly why Simsim was so nervous. 'As a cat I may have nine lives,' he reminded himself, stroking his whiskers, 'but this is my first and probably last hajj: I want to get things right first time. I probably won't have another chance!'

On the plane, Simsim had trimmed his claws, washed as he did before praying and put on the special long white cloth that he had brought with him. He wrapped it round his waist, tucked it in and threw the rest of it over his shoulder. The other hajjis had done that, too, and they all looked the same, wearing their ihram. 'That's how it should be!' mused Simsim. 'Allah doesn't care who's a Cool Cat or who's a Top Dog!'

Makka was a tail's length away from Jedda and hajjis kept calling out, 'Here I come!' getting louder and faster as they got closer to the city. Simsim had never ridden a camel before and it was fun to whiz past the donkeys, buses and people on foot. At times, he wished he had travelled by paw as the camel ride made the fur on his neck stand on end!

His guide in Makka had a bowl of cool, creamy milk waiting for him and greeted him, 'Assalamu aleikum!' Simsim touched his paw to his chest and replied, 'Wa aleikum salam!' Then the two of them went to hunt for the hotel.

The Ka'aba was beyond Simsim's wildest dreams. As the swirling crowds encircled the ancient stone, pressing forward to kiss it, Simsim felt every one of his whiskers tingling.

At Zamzam, there is a special spring and even before he could see or hear it, Simsim's tail began to quiver. The cheetah in him surged forth and he raced to the fresh water, outpacing the two-legged pilgrims.

All the hajjis were on Mount Arafat together and when they prayed silently, there wasn't a miaow to be heard for miles. 'A most welcome paws for thought!' Simsim chuckled. Tents went up all over the plain and a delicious smell of cooking wafted on the breeze. They served Simsim fish just the way he liked it – raw and with the head left on.

The next stop was Mina, and Simsim was already dreading having his head shaved. 'I know I'm supposed to be a baby, starting life again after hajj,' he thought, 'but kittens aren't born bald. And anyway, I've become very attached to my fur – or rather, my fur has become very attached to me!' Going round the Ka'aba again, Simsim's ears stuck out and he felt

a bit funny. He also felt funny leaving Makka: it had really been the experience of a lifetime and he felt a completely new cat.

The mice were lazing in the sun when Simsim's taxi turned the corner. 'D-rat!' they screeched and scuttled under floorboards for safety. Gradually, a few of the brave ventured out to explore and they caught a glimpse of something rare and wonderful: the transformation of Simsim! He had brought souvenirs of the hajj and special Muslim items from Makka and Mina. On a shelf was a model of the Ka'aba and decorative metal plaques on which the names of Allah were written in Arabic. On the big wall, in blue and green, hung a magnificent embroidered hanging, depicting the Prophet's mosque in Madinah. But what really made them gasp was the sight of Simsim himself, their arch-enemy, sitting cross-legged on his prayer mat, engrossed in reading the Qur'an from its stand. Wearing a prayer cap, he fingered beads of precious Tiger's Eye stones – one for each of the 99 names of Allah. 'That's some cat!' Farel exclaimed and scuttled back to tell the others.

'Many Muslims say that the hajj is the most important event of their life and really changes them deep down,' explained Faron, 'though how it happens is very complicated, well, compli-cat-ted, anyway! Perhaps we could shake tails and be friends. There is a very 'mice' custom of going to congratulate and welcome a hajji. Nefar, will you go on our behalf?'

'Not me! I know that cat too well.'
'What are you – a mouse or a man?'
'I'm alive and I'd like to keep it that way!'
'All right, who then?'

'Fara! Fara!' a group volunteered. 'She's good at that sort of thing!' They all agreed – all except Fara. Her frail body trembled and her tiny teeth chattered as they nudged her to the front. 'You could charm the birds off the trees!' Nefar remarked. 'And Simsim would adore that! There was a chorus of laughter and mousy smiles all round.

When Fara reached Simsim's room, he was in the same position – absolutely still, with his eyes closed. 'Let sleeping cats lie!' she thought to herself, tiptoeing reluctantly across the carpet. Simsim did not budge. 'Hmhm! Hmhm!' she coughed to attract his attention, sidling a little closer. 'Assa… Assalamu,' she stuttered. 'Assalamu aleikum!'

Simsim opened one eye, took one look at the tasty dinner in front of him and drew himself up to his full size. The petrified mouse recoiled in fright and a split second later the huge creature pounced. He struck once more but missed her again as she dodged behind the desk, her tiny heart pounding in her chest. She cowered there for a moment, trying to calm down and think clearly. 'What am I doing here?' she wondered. 'How could I be so stupid?' Before she could answer herself, she saw the monster's claws coming towards her and she knew she'd have to be on the run again. Scuttling along the wall, she spied a hole in the corner and dived in, the tip of her tail escaping the clutches of the feline foe by a hair's breadth. Fara heard him scream, 'Rats!' as she scampered along the narrow passageway, took a flying leap and landed breathless in the nest.

'He *prays* like a hajji,' she panted, 'but he *hunts* like a cat!'

****

Background and treatment

This story is an expansion and adaptation of a Syrian folktale about a cat that went to Makka. It is about not judging other people and about being sincere yourself. Because 'far' is Arabic for 'mouse', this version gives the mice names that have 'far' in them. 'Simsim' means 'sesame' and it used as a pet name for a cat in some Arabic-speaking communities.

Reflective questions

■ Why is the hajj a life-changing experience?

■ Was Simsim really a cat on the inside and a hajji on the outside? Or was he a hajji on the inside and a cat on the outside?

■ Is it important for people to be the same inside and out? If so, how?

■ Is it possible for people to consciously change their personality?

Growing up

Leaves rustled, mud squelched and twigs snapped. The three gardeners looked up, downed tools and scratched their heads as the Superintendent of Parks made an entrance through the shrubbery. Why couldn't their boss come along the paths like anyone else?

Common-or-garden Superpark had something important to say. 'I have to go to a meeting and I'll be off-site for some time. Can I rely on you to keep things going – or, should I say, growing?'

'Great!' thought Green Fingers, 'Here's a real chance to prove what I can do.'

'It'll be nice not to have to worry about work too much!' was Grow Bag's first reaction. 'I'm sick of all this raking and hoeing. I want to enjoy life!'

For Flower Pot, it was a totally different story. 'I don't know if I can cope without Superpark around. I haven't got a clue about this work. I'm told what to do and I get on with it.'

'The thing is,' Superpark continued, 'this park can't be allowed to turn into a wilderness just because I'm not here and I do *not* expect to come back and find everything's gone to seed, eh? Joke!'

Grow Bag, Green Fingers and Flower Pot exchanged pained looks and attempted a feeble laugh.

'I've got some rather special varieties of seed here and I'm trusting you to take good care of them.' The three gardeners heard the familiar rattle of dry seeds, as Superpark handed out the little paper packets. They were attracted by the brightly coloured pictures and squinted to read the small print. Their concentration was broken by a rustle of leaves and they caught the last glimpse of Superpark disappearing through the hedge.

Clutching the packets firmly, Flower Pot made straight for the shed where there was a wooden box on the top shelf. 'I don't want these getting damaged or stolen so I'll keep them under lock and key, and bolt the potting-shed door.'

Grow Bag figured out, 'If I get these into the ground quickly, I can leg it over to the swings and slides, and have a bit of fun before the park closes.' It really didn't take much time at all to scatter the seeds on the soil, sprinkle some moss peat over them and turn on the hose.

By then, Green Fingers was on the way back from the library with a book on how to look after delicate plants. It explained how important it is to be patient and gentle with young seedlings. It said that plants are like people because they both need tender loving care and that a good gardener believes deep down that something really wonderful can begin with a tiny speck.

Every day, on the way to the skate ramps or the adventure playground, Grow Bag would enjoy seeing a few shoots gradually turning into fully-fledged plants and would help them along by pulling out a weed or two.

People strolling through the grounds always stopped to admire Green Fingers' glorious plantations where all sorts of life were flourishing. Green Fingers tended it almost day and night-weeding and watering, fertilising and fussing...

And all the while, Flower Pot stood guard outside the shed to keep off vandals.

The three gardeners had almost forgotten about Superpark until the day they saw the hedge moving again...

'I've still got your seeds!' exclaimed Flower Pot. 'Nothing's happened to them since you gave them to me.'

Superpark didn't need to be shown what Grow Bag and Green Fingers had done. 'One of the things decided at the meeting was the need for our parks and gardens to grow. You've got a few nice things going there, Grow Bag, and I'd like to put you in charge of our allotment project. What do you say?' Grow Bag nodded vigorously.

'Green Fingers, this is too beautiful for words. Would you take on responsibility for new developments?' They shook hands.

Flower Pot stood waiting, too choked to speak, with a sad but hopeful expression. 'Don't worry, Flower Pot. You've still got your job here and I know what you're thinking,' said Superpark. 'You've kept the seeds safe and dry but I asked you to care for them. Seeds aren't meant to stay seeds. They're supposed to fill the world with flowers and fruit, with beautiful colours and delicious scents. All you've done is stop them growing.'

***

Background and treatment

Jesus told many parables to help people understand things in life that are difficult or complicated. A parable is usually about something quite ordinary and familiar. Sometimes the storyteller explains how the complicated thing is like the ordinary thing; but sometimes the storyteller leaves it to the listeners to work it out for themselves!

This story is adapted from the 'parable of the talents', which is recorded in the Bible (Matthew 25 and Luke 19). A 'talent' was a sum of money and we get the word for someone's ability from this story. But this modern version has seeds instead of talents.

Reflective questions

- Did Grow Bag really care for the seeds more than Flower Pot? Should Green Fingers have not worked so hard on the seeds and perhaps spent more time with the family or enjoying hobbies? Was Common-or-garden Superpark fair to the gardeners in the end?

- What is the relationship between growth and risk?

- What do you think the parable is really about?

A Dream of a Place

Solomon was one of those people who paid a lot of attention to their dreams. Every morning he went through in his mind what had happened in his sleep. Often his dreams made no sense at all to him and he would ask other people what they meant.

Although King Solomon was supposed to be wise, there were actually many choices he found hard to make. What was bothering him was where to build the Temple. Obviously it had to be somewhere that everybody could get to easily. It had to be in beautiful surroundings... but there was something else. The place itself had to say something about what the Temple was for, what the whole idea was of worshipping God. One morning, Solomon leapt out of bed and knew the exact spot...

On the top of Mount Moriah there was a field owned by two brothers. They got on well and worked hard to make things grow. If they had any problems, they talked them over, and they always made decisions together. 'What shall we plant this year?' they'd say, and they'd sort it out. Whenever they had to buy something for their field, they paid half each and at the end of the harvest they divided the crops evenly.

The only difference between them was the way they lived. One of them had a house in a corner of the field where he lived on his own with just a few animals. His brother was married, had several children ranging from babies to teenagers, and they lived in the house in the opposite corner of the field.

One evening, the single brother wondered, 'Why do my brother and I get the same? He has several mouths to feed but there's only one of me! I know, in the morning I'll take him some of the crops from my barn... oh, but he'll never accept them. I can just hear him saying, 'Fair's fair! We put the same in. We take the same out.' I'll have to get it to him when he's not looking. As soon as it's dark, I'll fill a sack in my barn, trudge across the field and over the hill to *his* barn. Then I'll empty it into his granary and slip quietly back across the field. He'll never know how it got there and he'll have a lovely surprise.'

At exactly the same moment, the married brother wondered, 'Why do my brother and I get the same? I have a wonderful family. My wife and I care for our children while they are young and we know they will care for us when we are old. But my brother lives all alone. I wonder if he is lonely. I know, in the morning I'll take him some of the crops from my barn ... oh, but he'll never accept them. I can just hear him saying, 'Fair's fair! We put the same in. We take the same out.' I'll have to get it to him when he's not looking. As soon as it's dark, I'll fill a sack in my barn, trudge across the field and over the hill to his barn. Then I'll empty it into his granary and slip quietly back across the field. He'll never know how it got there and he'll have a lovely surprise.'

At dead of night, each brother set out for the opposite corner, with a heavy sack on his back. Each crept into his brother's barn, laid down his gift, silently closed the door behind him and hurried back in secret.

But when they returned to their own barn, each brother found a sack still there. Utterly mystified, he loaded up once more and began the journey back to his brother's store. Again and again, there was always one more sack.

Up and down, back and forth they went, bearing loads of love through the night.

As dawn broke, the two brothers crossed on the top of the hill and saw each other face to face. Realising what had happened, they started to laugh. Then their hearts filled up, tears flowed down their cheeks, and they hugged and danced till morning.

***

Background and treatment

Many Jewish stories that look for meanings are *midrashim*. A *midrash* is a story that tries to answer people's questions about life in general or about just one thing.

King Solomon built the Jewish temple in Jerusalem about 3000 years ago. Centuries later, when some Jews were wondering why their Temple was built in a particular place, this *midrash* was told.

Reflective questions

- Did you have any idea that the two brothers would do the same for each other? What did you think would happen *in the end*?

- Should everyone get the same in life?

- Why do people sometimes want a special place for worship? What made the place that Solomon chose so special? What else might happen in a place to make it be remembered as somewhere special?

Taking sides

Thwack! Crunch! Boff! Zap! Aaah!

Fighting had been very fierce for several weeks and from early morning the two sides had been giving each other a particularly serious hammering. Glares were exchanged, with menacing eyes and bared teeth, as the warriors engaged in the most desperate struggle of their lives – a fight to the finish... Winning was everything!

The sun beat down mercilessly, sweat poured off the soldiers' brows and their bodies flagged with exhaustion. By evening, the battlefield was strewn with the defeated and the dying. The corpses and the collapsed lay side by side, overlapping or even heaped together on the ground. The air was filled with the stench of blood and the mingled cries of pain.

As dusk fell, a lone figure was silhouetted against the sky, treading carefully, and weaving in and out of the piles of bodies. On a thick strap around Khaneeya's neck was slung a huge leather bottle and as he passed each soldier he called out, 'Water! Water! Who needs water?' Some of the injured could barely raise an eyebrow. Some could only manage a limp wave of the hand or a tired, aching moan.

At every sign of life, Khaneeya poured a few precious drops into the mouths of the wounded. Many of them revived and his cheerful, loving words brought them hope.

But Khaneeya's comrades in the Sikh army saw what he was doing. 'Hey, Khaneeya!' they yelled, 'What do you think you're doing?' He pretended not to hear. 'Oi! You're quenching their blokes' thirst not just our lot... Have you gone over to the other side or can't you tell the difference?'

'I know who's who, all right,' replied Khaneeya, carrying on.

'Look, Khaneeya,' said one of the bigger men, 'if you don't stop helping the other lot...!'

One of the other Sikhs put a hand on his shoulder. 'Don't mess with that bloke. I reckon Guru Gobind Singh should work it all out. He's chief around here.' They all agreed.

'My saint-soldiers,' said Guru Gobind Singh in a warm, gentle voice, 'the battle is over for the day but you look ready to kill!'

'He's a traitor! Or else he's gone mad! He's dishing out water to Sikhs who have fainted *and* to 'them'. We slog our guts out all day, knocking them out, and he gets them going again so they can do us in tomorrow! What are you going to do about him?'

The guru was not the kind of person who jumped to conclusions. 'I'm not going to 'do' anything about him,' he replied. 'I think I'll stroll over and have a little chat.' He was not called 'true king' for nothing.

'There is a rumour, Khaneeya, that you have been helping our enemies. What do you have to say for yourself?'

'It's not true!'

'Look at me: are you telling me that you have not been helping the enemy?'

'I don't *have* any enemies... I see looks of pain, I hear cries of agony and I feel they're just people, children of the same God who made me. They need water, too.'

'Oh, Khaneeya,' said Guru Gobind Singh, hugging him tightly, his eyes filling with tears. 'What a splendid person you are! A really wonderful Sikh! We're fighting this war to hang on to our faith and our faith tells us everyone is equal, with a right to life and the freedom to find God in their own way. What you did was really marvellous because you showed that feeling was maybe even more important than winning the war. When you go back, take this from me,' and he handed him ointment and bandages. 'I want to call you 'Bhai' because you are a real brother...'

Bhai Khaneeya thanked the guru, 'But what about the rumour?'

'Don't worry about the others!' Guru Gobind Singh grinned. 'I can handle them!'

As Bhai Khaneeya headed back to the battlefield, Guru Gobind Singh summoned the rest of his men. 'When an army is fighting us and our religion, they are enemies but, once they lie wounded, they are just humans, I would even say, our friends.'

His eyes scanned the plain and there was Bhai Khaneeya, kneeling on the ground and dressing the wounds of a man from the other side.

***

Background and treatment

Sikhs love to tell stories from the lives of the ten gurus, the teachers of their tradition. About 300 years ago, the last human guru, Guru Gobind Singh created the *khalsa*, the Sikh community. The guru who came after him and did not die was the Sikh scripture, the *Guru Granth Sahib*.

Reflective questions

■ How might Guru Gobind Singh have handled the others? What might he have said to them to make them believe Bhai Khaneeya was doing the best thing?

■ Is it right for a group of people to fight to defend their religion if another group is attacking it? Or should someone who is religious never fight at all?

■ Which is it more important to care about – all humanity or our own community?

Firing a shot

When Malunkyaputta heard the Buddha teaching, the way he saw life changed. He decided to become one of the Buddha's followers and live as a monk. But something else happened later that again changed the way that Malunkyaputta saw life.

Like other monks, Malunkyaputta spent several hours a day in quiet and concentrated thought. One afternoon, when he rose from his meditation, his head was buzzing with ideas and questions. He was desperate for answers that would help calm his mind and so he went to see the Buddha.

'I've got a lot on my mind, Blessed One,' he began. 'I've been wondering whether the universe will last for ever or some day end... whether space goes on and on or just stops... whether the soul and the body are really the same or different... There are many things like this that you've never really explained and I don't like that one bit! It's not fair! If you know the answers, then please just tell me. And if you don't know the answers, then why don't you just say 'I don't know'?'

'Malunkyputta,' replied the Buddha calmly, 'Did I ever say to you, 'Be my follower and I will explain these things to you'?'

'Well, no...'

'And, Malunkyaputta, did you ever say to me, 'I'll be your follower and then you'll explain these things to me'?'

'Well, no...'

'And I'm saying to you now, Malunkyaputta,' the Buddha went on, 'that I'm *not* saying, 'Be my follower and I'll explain these things to you.' And you're not even saying to me, either, 'I'll be your follower and then you'll explain these things to me.' Let me tell you, Malunkyaputta, anyone who says, 'I won't be a follower of the Buddha until he explains these things to me' would die before the things were explained.'

Malunkyaputta could see that the Buddha hadn't gone back on his word. He didn't have the answers to his questions but then the Buddha had never promised him those sorts of answers – and he had never really asked them before. Then the Buddha said something that made him think that he had been asking the wrong questions all the time!

'Imagine that someone's been shot by a poisoned arrow,' the Buddha said. 'And they're taken to a doctor to have it removed. Just imagine them saying, 'I won't have this arrow taken out until I know what kind of person shot it at me... what their name is... whether they're tall, short or of average height... what colour their skin is... where they come from... what kind of bow was used... or bowstring... what type of arrow... what kinds of feathers there were on the arrow... what the arrow head was made of..."

Put like that, it did seem ridiculous to Malunkyaputta! And it was obvious that these would be really stupid questions to ask in a situation like that. The first and most important thing to do would be to get the arrow out!

'A person like that would die never having their questions answered,' the Buddha concluded. 'It's just the same with your questions, Malunkyaputta. Whatever ideas anyone has, they can't get away from the fact that there is sadness and suffering in life – and there's a way to end them. That's what I've been trying to tell you all the time we've been together. And the reason that I don't answer your questions,' the Buddha said simply, 'is that there's no point!'

Some time later Malunkyaputta went to see the Buddha again. But this time he asked the Buddha something else – to help him understand suffering and how it can be ended. And Malunkyaputta himself became a holy one, worthy of the respect that people gave him.

•••

Background and treatment

The story of Malunkyaputta is well known to Buddhists. He was a monk who asked the Buddha five pairs of questions.

The Buddha was very practical. Once, he took some leaves in his hand and asked some monks who were his followers, 'Where are there more leaves – in my hand or in the whole forest?' They replied, 'There are hardly any leaves in your hand but lots of leaves in the forest!'

He explained, 'The leaves in my hand are like what I have told you and the leaves in the forest are like what I haven't told you. What I haven't said is more than what I have said! That's because I've only told you things that'll help you live a good and happy life. Everything else is just empty ideas that aren't certain and don't get us anywhere.'

Reflective questions

■ In what ways are the questions that the person who has been shot asks about the bow similar to the questions that Malunkyaputta asks? In what ways are these two kinds of questions different?

■ What are the advantages and disadvantages of having leader who has a strong influence on the way that his or her followers think?

■ Why is it important to think well in order to live well?

■ Is it pointless to ask questions that have no answers?

Just a Drop

'You worry too much, Shuvi. It's dead simple. All we had to do was find our favourite thing,' Feleh explained.

'No, we had to get the most *precious* thing in all the world,' Shuvi corrected him.

'Same difference!'

'Yeah? Why did we have to do it, anyway?'

'Search me. I'm not God, am I?' replied Feleh, sounding obvious.

'The thing is,' interrupted Zedka, 'we've all brought something, so let's take a look. Bags be first!' Out of her backpack she pulled a small square of white cloth with a red mark in the middle. She opened it out on her lap and smoothed it down.

'Strawberry jam – yummy!' guessed Shuvi.

'Ha! ha!' came a sarcastic laugh.

'Tomato sauce...!' suggested Feleh. 'You had some lovely chips and got ketchup all over your hanky!'

'Oh, honestly! It's blood!'

'Me next!' piped Feleh. Taking care to keep it upright, he brought out of his satchel a test tube that he held firmly between his thumb and forefinger. It contained a small amount of yellow fluid and had a cork stopper.

'Is it from some scientific experiment?' Zedka wondered.

'No, but you're close.'

'Oh, I know,' cried Shuvi. 'It's a magic potion!'

But Feleh dismissed her idea with a wave of the hand. 'It's a shot of vaccine!'

Shuvi had to keep her lunchbox absolutely level and carry it very steadily. She took out a minute, round dish, placed it gently on her palm and held out her hand flat. The other two stared at it for a moment, barely making out that there was something clear in the bottom.

'Don't tell me you've been catching rain!' enquired Feleh cheekily.

'Or stealing holy water!' Zedka accused jokingly.

'Not at all! It's a tear!'

The three of them sat back and pondered their various finds: it was strange they had all chosen small drops of something; even stranger that they had been unable to guess what each other's choice was; and strangest of all that no one else could imagine why they'd chosen that particular treasure.

Had they come up with the things that were actually precious to God, they needed to know. How could they find out? Maybe God had let them be free to decide for themselves and would say that whatever they chose – and really meant – was right... Did it matter that they were different? Can you logically have more than one *most* precious thing? Why had God sent them off to find the most valuable thing of all? Surely God already knew the answer... So what was this game all about? What would anyone get out of it? And what, in the end, would God make of their funny little efforts?

Round and round they went, turning so many questions over in their mind. 'Maybe there are some things about God that we'll never understand,' Shuvi reflected after a while.

But Feleh spoke for all three of them when he exclaimed, 'I've got brain pain!'

'Why don't we just come out with it and tell each other *why* we collected the drops?' said Zedka, trying to be practical. 'Who knows, perhaps we've all hit on the same idea. If we haven't, maybe we could vote on the one most precious thing out of all our precious three...'

They nodded in agreement and leaned back to show she could go first. Zedka spread out her blood-stained piece of gauze and began her tale.

'In a South American village, high up in the mountains, the life of the peasants is a bitter struggle. They are downtrodden by wealthy landowners who charge them high rents and take a greedy share of the crops they grow. Foreign businessmen make them work long hours for low wages in dangerous mines or dirty factories. 'Enough of this!' declared a young man one day. He was the eldest son in his family. 'Our government is full of crooks. They steal from the poor to give to the rich. Wherever we turn for help, the door is slammed in our face! There has to be a better life!'

'There is, my boy,' his mother replied. 'It is beyond the grave. We have been told our reward will be in heaven.'

'They only tell us that to keep us quiet, to stop us complaining! It's no good, Mama! There are other young men who think like me. We're going to fight. We'll change it all, you'll see!' Putting on his soldier's cap, he kissed his mother good-bye and ran down the mountainside, brave and free. The next she saw of him was when a donkey came clip-clop up the hill, bringing his body home. 'Sweet Mama...' he called softly before he died.'

'And here,' Zedka announced, 'is his final drop of blood – the most precious thing in all the world.'

Gripping the test tube between thumb and forefinger, Feleh cleared his throat and described his scene.

'In Central Africa there was a clinic – the only one for hundreds of miles – which was run single-handed by a devoted nurse. Though conditions were hard and resources scarce, no one in need of her help was ever turned away and she worked tirelessly, coaxing her patients back to health or bringing comfort to the dying. Not once did she complain of the hardship and not once did she have a selfish thought. Whenever she was asked how long she had been at the clinic, she would smile and say sweetly, 'This is my life!'

One day an epidemic struck the whole area. Entire families died from the disease and her clinic soon became overcrowded. Day and night, she nursed her patients, often tired and weak herself. She offered them water and mopped their fevered brows, saving the little vaccine there was for the babies and children. Before long, she too was in the grip of the same sickness and she collapsed in the corner of the ward. All night, as the fever raged in her infected body, she fought for her life but in the morning, with a prayer on her lips, she died.'

'And here,' Feleh announced, 'is the vaccine that could have saved her – the most precious thing in all the world.'

Finally, Shuvi placed the dish gently on the flat of her hand and told her story.

'There was a well-known thief in Eastern Europe. Not trusting anyone, he worked alone and at night. Everyone knew he was a burglar but could never prove it as he was too good at his job.

All his adult life he had never known anything but crime: he had snatched handbags, picked pockets, robbed banks, forged cheques and held up trains.

And then, one snowy night, he went out on a job. There was a house he had had his eye on for some time. Covering his tracks, he crept into the yard and down the alley at the side. He could drop in through a window without being noticed. A drainpipe was perfectly placed and he scaled it in no time but just then he heard sounds coming from inside. Edging his way from one sill to the next, he peered through a gap in the curtains into a room full of happiness: the grandmother was knitting and the grandfather was singing at the piano; children played together on the rug; the father was piling logs onto the fire and in an armchair the mother was feeding her baby. Their closeness and contentment touched him deeply, and there was a look on their faces and a sound in their voices that reminded him of his own family he had loved so dearly when he was a boy and the good, simple life he had left behind.

Filled with regret, he turned away and jumped back into the yard. Overcome with shame, he crouched down and wept.'

'And here,' Shuvi announced, 'is a single tear of a soul that is truly sorry – the most precious thing in all the world.'

***

Background and treatment

This is based on a Jewish folktale, in which God sends three angels to find out what is precious in the world.

This story is relevant to *Yom Kippur*, the festival for feeling sorry and of saying sorry to people and to God. Jews pray about three things at that time: *tzedekah* (fairness), *t'filah* (prayer) and *t'shuvah* (changing for the better). In this modern version of the story, the children's names are taken from these three things.

Reflective questions

■ In what ways are the three children' finds – of something precious – similar? In what ways are they different?

■ Did the children need to choose one or can they have three most precious things?

■ Which of the children's finds is most precious to you?

■ What was the most precious question the children asked?

What It's Worth

The sun had hardly risen and already it was stronger than anyone could bear. For months there had been no rain and the land was dry, their water cisterns were dry, and their throats were dry. If nothing happened soon, maybe even their hope would dry out.

The crops had long since been eaten and nothing would grow in the cracked soil of Madinah, the city so loved by the Prophet Muhammad – the first home of the Muslim community.

Before the famine, Madinah was an oasis in the desert, a fresh and vibrant spot in a stretch of scorching sand as far as the eye could see.

Now shops were shut, stalls folded away and merchants long gone. The town that had once been bustling and noisy was deserted and eerie, and the only sounds to be heard were the stirring calls to prayer five times a day and the pitiful cries of starving babies.

For a while, wealthy families still had water from their private wells and had laid in stocks of food, but they too ran out. Lounging under the shade of palm trees, they could only dream they were sipping cool drinks, sucking slices of juicy melon and chewing dates.

From beneath a canopy on the flat roof of her home, Laila's eye caught something tiny shimmering on the horizon. She leapt up in excitement, pointing and shrieking, 'Look!'

They *did* look but saw nothing.

'It's just a mirage!' sneered Laila's brother. But Laila was right: making its way over the sand dunes was the heavily laden camel caravan of Utman, the third calif, a rich and well respected businessman who had been on a shopping expedition.

'We're saved!' shouted Laila's thrilled parents, and by the time they had reached the gates of the city, the whole neighbourhood had heard of Laila's sighting and were following close behind. Some even ran out through the gates and over the burning hot sand to meet Utman.

'What did you get?' they clamoured to know, tugging at his kaftan and almost pulling him off his camel.

'I'll take the lot!' pressed one of the richest men in Madinah.

'No way!' replied Utman, with a wave of the hand.

'I'll double the offer!' shouted another.

'No chance!'

'We'll pay you *three* times what it cost you!' bid the sisters who dealt in spices.

'No. Sorry!' responded Utman, with a perplexed smile.

'I can raise that to four!' proclaimed a metalsmith, pushing his way to the front of the crowd.

'Nothing doing, I'm afraid!' Utman insisted.

'Five!'

'Not interested!'

'I'll go up to six times what the load is worth!' said the silk trader. 'How would you like it? Cloth? Perfume? Gems? Gold?'

'Madam, I don't care how you pay because you are *not* paying,' Utman explained firmly.

'Now here's an offer you can't refuse!' boasted a jeweller, weighing words carefully. 'Seven, S-E-V-E-N times what you paid, cash in hand!'

By now, with crowds pressing all around, Utman had reached the archway into Madinah and dismounted. 'Look, you can make me offers until the camels come home, but this food is not for sale simply because it belongs to someone else who is paying me *ten times* what it's worth.'

'Ten?' they gasped.

'That's right. Now would you please let me pass?'

There was a stunned silence. Whoever could it be that could pay ten times what the goods were worth? Surely there was no one in Madinah richer than them. The only way to find out was to follow Utman. They caught up with him and tagged along behind as he headed for downtown Madinah where he unloaded his camel bags onto the streets.

'*Allah* is great!' he called. 'Come to eat!' and he handed out armfuls of food to the poor. It was beyond their wildest dreams and Utman saw sad faces changed by looks of surprise, smiles of thankfulness and tears of joy.

'Liar! Cheat!' shouted the wealthy mob behind him with angry eyes and clenched fists. 'No one bought it for ten times more! You deserve to be...!'

'Allah is the someone!' Utman explained. 'Look at the difference it's made to these beloved people. Don't you remember that it says in our Holy *Qur'an* that if you do something good, Allah will reward that ten times over.'

In the distance, the *muezzin* was calling from the *minar* at the set time: 'Come to prayer! Come to success!'

***

Background and treatment

About 1400 year ago, when the Prophet Muhammad died, four califs – one after the other – became leader of the Muslim community. Muslims have kept alive the stories of the califs and their example of good living.

Reflective questions

■ What made Utman refuse the wonderful offers for his goods? Did you have any idea of the 'someone' who had already bought it all? Had it really all been bought?

■ Are poor people more deserving than rich people?

■ In what ways would Utman get paid by Allah ten times over? Do people usually get rewarded for the good things they do?

Something in the Air

The moment Mishka opened her eyes, she knew there was something wrong. Her pillow was slimy to the touch, making her flesh creep, and the air seemed foggy and dank. Half hoping she was just dreaming, she stretched her arms and yawned. It made her tongue go sticky and warts appeared on her lips. 'Ugh!' She sniffed the air but her nostrils and throat seized up and a sharp pain gripped her chest. Her head started spinning and she felt sick in the pit of her stomach.

Sobbing only made her head hurt more and she began wondering if there was something drilling or banging inside her brain. 'I'm not staying here!' Still dizzy, she staggered across the room to the window: there was a swirling mist so thick and steamy that she could barely see the rest of Vrindavan, though across the street she could hear people bustling about and calling to each other. In the distance, the waters of the Yamuna were turbulent.

Downstairs, Mishka's parents were in a state of distress. 'It's coming up from the river, enveloping everything. We're practically suffocating,' they wailed. But Mishka just wanted to know why!

'There she goes again, asking questions!' her mother complained. 'Some things you're better off not knowing!'

'I do want to know everything,' thought Mishka. 'They treat me like a baby! And I have a right to know what keeps sending up these wafts of putrid air. . .' and she stormed out.

Everyone else in the village seemed to be spluttering and scratching. Women's saris were discoloured and whitewashed houses were stained by the smog. There were babies with weeping sores and children with streaming eyes. Adults had swollen joints and the elderly had blistered skin.

Mishka decided she would keep her eyes and ears open, and gradually she was able to piece together part of the story. It seemed that a serpent had swum into the river Yamuna, just where it widens out to form a lake. He was so vile that he even contaminated the air and birds flying overhead, overcome by the fumes, crashed into the torrent. Kaliya had more heads and tails than anyone could count and when he thrashed about, he created such a commotion that the land around the Yamuna was drenched and nothing could stay alive – trees, crops, animals, even people...

Terror struck the villagers' hearts as agitated voices came from the field between Vrindavan and the river. Was Kaliya coming to attack? Surely he could not survive out of the water.

Panting and gasping, some cowherds were racing towards the anxious, huddled crowds... but they were beaming. 'As we were tending our cows, we noticed the unmistakable footprints of Krishna. He has come to us...'

'All thanks and praise to Lord Krishna!' uttered an ecstatic old woman. 'He will always rescue those who are devoted to him and drive away all evil from their life!'

Passing through the fields with the others, Mishka saw clearly enough the special marks of Krishna's feet – a flag, a bow, a shell – but they also met his mother, Yashoda. She was in tears. Her husband, Nanda, was trying to comfort her but he, too, was overcome with worry and grief and their other son stood by helplessly. 'We can tell he's in danger,' wept Yashoda. 'Where is he? What's he doing?'

They might have known... Krishna had already climbed a *kadamba* tree – the only one that had not withered on the riverbank – and its tiny, round, yellow flowers framed his face, making him look even younger than he was.

The spectators gasped when Krishna suddenly leapt and plunged into the water. He flapped his arms, kicked his legs and created such a splash that the Yamuna flooded its banks. Frolicking in the water, Krishna looked like a playful little elephant enjoying a cool dip but Kaliya soon sensed that a force had invaded his territory. His many heads rose up above the water and with each cruel, ugly mouth he spat and hissed. Writhing about and thwacking the surface of the river with his tails, he created a terrifying thud. Then he lunged forward, grabbed Krishna with his powerful coils and gripped him tight.

The earth began to tremble, meteors crashed through the sky and shivers ran down everyone's spine.

Instinctively, Yashoda rushed to protect her child and Nanda and Balarama had to pull her back, afraid she would swallow some poison.

Mishka loved Krishna so much that she felt she, too, was struggling with evil. She thought about all the horrible things she had ever done – or just thought – and was filled with shame. She was sorry she had had horrid thoughts about her Ba and Baba at home earlier. 'Why did I have to be so nasty? If Krishna can get rid of Kaliya,' she decided, 'I can get rid of all the nasty things in me.' For two hours it went on, Krishna in the clutches of Kaliya and Mishka in the clutches of her own guilt. Then, suddenly she felt an elbow nudging her. 'Look!' A different kind of power was coursing through Krishna. His body started to expand so much that Kaliya's strength was stretched to the limit. He strained to hold the baby Lord but he could not: the coils slackened, his stranglehold was released and Krishna slipped from his grasp.

Unconquered and with his eyes blazing in fury, Kaliya spread out his hoods, blew poison from his mouths and exhaled fire from his nostrils. Then it was Krishna's turn to act. Bouncing from one head to another, he stunned and confused the wicked monster, who spat out wildly but missed every time. Krishna pounced again. Once more the creature emitted a noxious substance and once more his opponent, with nimble feet, outwitted him. Higher and higher Krishna leapt until he was dancing on the tallest hood. In a last attempt to defeat his destroyer, the enraged serpent thrust at him with all his vicious heads at once but Krishna was just out of reach. Exhausted, the multi-headed snake finally surrendered and slumped into the water.

Still hopping sprightly on Kaliya's highest head, Krishna took out his flute and, with his face all aglow, he played the sweetest tune the exultant villagers had ever heard. Humiliated, Kaliya slunk down the river and out of sight.

At once, the water became clear and blue, and fish swam about freely. Grass turned lush and green, and trees blossomed again. 'Evil has gone! God is good!' shouted the people. As Lord Krishna touched dry land, his worshippers garlanded him with flowers and spread petals at his feet.

'Mishka? Mishka?' a frantic mother was calling. Mishka would have known that voice anywhere.

'I'm here, Ba! What's the matter?'

'Oh, thank goodness you're all right...' panted her mother, pushing through the crowds. 'I've been so worried about you all day. You just went off without saying where you were going and I was afraid maybe you'd, you know...'

'Oh, Ba!' said Mishka, stroking her mother's cheek. 'I'm...'

'What, Mishka?' she asked softly.

'Oh nothing, Ba,' she replied and gave her a little squeeze. 'It's all right!'

***

Background
Hindus believe that God appears in life in many different ways. As Vishnu, who preserves the world, God can take the form of Krishna and many Hindus worship Krishna as God. There is a tradition of stories in which Krishna likes playing and is small but strong.

The story of Krishna defeating Kaliya may also be understood as a modern myth or a metaphor for the defeat of evil in our world. The evil may be inner or outer, that is, inner and outer evil

Reflective questions
■ Do we all have bad things inside us that we feel ashamed of? How did they get there? Can we get rid of them by ourselves? How? Does it help to have stories of God removing evil from the world?

■ If we are unhappy or unwell, does it help to know why?

■ Do we have a right to know everything?

■ What do people fear today in the way that people in the story feared Kaliya?

■ What might Krishna and Kaliya represent? What form does the evil emitted by Kaliya take? What form might the defeat of evil take?

■ Why does Mishka feel confident that she will be safe?

The Stonecutter

Once upon a time, thousands of years ago in ancient China, there was a stonecutter. He was irritable and bitter, always complaining about his bad luck.

One day he walked past the mansion of a wealthy businessman, and as usual began complaining. As he glanced at the fine carriages in the courtyard, and saw all the important people standing around, he was full of envy. 'How wonderful and powerful that man is,' he thought. 'I wish I could be like that! Then I wouldn't have to spend all my time cutting and shaping stone.'

To his enormous surprise, he suddenly found himself changed into a wealthy businessman. He had great wealth and power, and was surrounded by luxury. But one day he saw an important government official going past his house, surrounded by attendants and escorted by troops of soldiers. As the procession went down the street, everyone in the city bowed low in respect.

'Oh if only I could be a government official, with everyone respecting me,' thought the man. 'That would be much better than being just a businessman. I could really make things happen.'

At that moment he was changed into a government official. He was carried everywhere in a handsome sedan chair, and all the people of the city bowed down to him.

The weather was particularly hot and uncomfortable. From his stuffy sedan chair, he looked up at the sun high in the sky. It shone there so proudly, totally unaffected by anything else. 'Oh if only I could be the sun,' he thought. 'Then I wouldn't be sweaty and uncomfortable and nothing would stop me from being contented.'

At that moment he was changed into the sun. He shone down fiercely onto the countryside, and was delighted that many people cursed him for scorching their crops. But a dark grey cloud moved between him and the earth, and his light could no longer reach the land below.

'How very powerful that cloud is,' he thought. 'If only I could be a cloud. I wouldn't be thwarted then by other things.'

He was changed into a rain cloud, and he took great pleasure in causing floods all over the country. But one day he found himself being blown all over the place by a forceful wind. 'Oh if only I could be the wind!' he thought. 'Then I could really throw my weight around. I could move, push and shove – I could do anything.'

He was changed into the wind, and he roared and blew and moved all kinds of things from one place to another. But one day he came up against something that would not shift, however strongly he blew. It was a great towering rock. 'Oh, if only I could be that unmovable rock,' he thought. 'Then absolutely nothing could push me around.'

He was changed into a great rock, and felt extremely powerful and unmovable. But then he heard the knock, knock, knock of a hammer hitting a chisel, and he realised with terror that he was himself being chipped away.

'So there is someone or something more powerful even than a towering rock,' he thought. 'Who or what on earth can it be?' He looked down. At the base of the towering rock, like a mere tiny insect, he could see a man with a hammer and chisel, chipping, breaking, shaping, carving.

It was a stonecutter.

***

Background and treatment

This is a Chinese story in the Tao tradition, which places a strong emphasis on acceptance and creative passivity, as distinct from aggressive activity arising from a desire to change and control events and situations.

Reflective questions

■ What might the stonecutter's 'bad luck' be and why might he be irritable and bitter?

■ In what ways are other people's lives unsatisfying?

■ What is the stonecutter really looking for?

■ How does the stonecutter benefit from seeing the world from different standpoints?

■ What does the stonecutter come to realise at the end? Did he find what he was looking for? Is it wise or unwise to want to be someone else?

Cup Final

Miri and Jess stared at each other in amazement, pinched themselves to make sure they were not dreaming and read the e-mail again.

To: jesseandmiriamstone@vesselgardens7.glastonbury.org

Subject: CONGRATULATIONS!!!

If you are Jesse and Miriam Stone of 7 Vessel Gardens, Glastonbury, your entry in the football competition came TOP! All five questions were answered correctly and your spot the ball was the most accurate ever recorded!

You are the winners of the first prize – a mystery tour in the specially designed ***TEMPLE OF QUEST*** that will transport you to seven major world sites!

And there's MORE!!! You could win the ***STAR PRIZE*** if you discover a hidden cup or bowl. You only have to ask the right question to unlock the secret!

But you must be ready to start NOW!!!

It was the most exciting thing that had ever happened to Miri and Jess, and they could hardly believe their good luck. They had always wanted the chance to see the world and the Temple of Quest sounded intriguing. Perhaps it will be like one of those time-ships in science fiction programmes, they wondered. Yet they were puzzled by the extra challenge they had been set – about something that looked like a cup or a bowl. 'That could be anything,' Miri remarked. 'But maybe the Temple of Quest will take us to it,' she added, trying to be helpful. 'And anyway, if they blot the football out of the photo of a match and we managed to guess where it would have been, surely we can find a glass or a dish! I'm much more bothered by the questions we have to ask. I don't normally go around quizzing coffee mugs or washing-up bowls!'

The Temple of Quest turned out to be a ball of smoky glass that bounced along Vessel Gardens. It had nothing inside but the number five flashed on the top all the time until it landed and Jess thought they had gone around the corner.

There were not, in fact, still in Glastonbury but outside a church in Guatemala. In front was a huge crucifix, bearing the carved figure of Christ dying. They could hear singing and a guitar being played in the church. Underneath a brightly coloured painting of Jesus feeding the five thousand with only five small loaves, the priest was celebrating Mass on the altar. 'This is my blood which is shed for you...' he proclaimed and in both hands he held high a silver goblet. They wondered if that was the cup but had to wait until the Mass had ended to find out.

'The Mass is a mystery – we feel it – it's hard to understand,' the priest explained, 'but Jesus did know he was going to die and at a special supper with his best friends, he picked up his wine glass and said, 'I'm pouring out my blood for you!' We say that at the Mass.'

He must have known what Miri and Jess were thinking because he went on, 'We put *wine* in the cup – not blood – but we believe that the spirit of the wine changes into the spirit of Christ's blood. Some people say Jesus' cup was used to collect drops of his actual blood and then put in a secret place... You would like to find Jesus' *actual* cup?' The priest smiled, laid his hands on their heads and continued, 'The chalice we use in the Mass is simply the same shape as the cup from which Jesus drank and into which his blood dripped. His cup was full of suffering. To understand that, you have to go out into the world. Unless you do, you won't find the solution to the mystery in here.'

'Then what is your church for?' Miri asked.

'God bless you, children!'

By now, the Temple of Quest was bobbing up and down in the town square and they climbed back in. It was another short trip and they had to stoop a little not to bump into the strings of brightly coloured lanterns that looked enchanting against the twilight sky. 'Welcome to The Good Luck Garden!' said the old man and he pointed to some cushions by a low table. As he poured them steaming tea from a blue and white porcelain teapot decorated with dragons, he noticed Jess staring, and Jess noticed that he noticed! Embarrassed, Jess mused, 'I notice there aren't many leaves in this kind of tea!'

'I don't need leaves: I'm not a fortune-teller,' the old man joked. 'There is no magic in this tea, though it is made according to an ancient Chinese recipe – simple but secret – using herbs, to promote long life and well being. I drink five cups a day and have great mental powers and inner calm.'

'How do you find peace of mind?' Jesse wanted to know.

'Be happy in your search!' was the reply.

'Back to the bubble!' piped Miri. 'We blew that one, too! But this next place I've seen on TV – they have baseball here!'

'Doesn't look like a sports stadium to me. More like an outdoor music hall,' Jess replied but just then the clown act finished, the audience exploded with laughter and applause, and the announcer came back onto the stage. 'And now, ladies and gentlemen, will you welcome back to the Hollywood Bowl our stars for tonight, The Bunch of Five! Yeah!' Shrieks, whistles and loud clapping brought the quintuplets on and the band struck up. 'Just look at those costumes and face paint!' exclaimed Jess. 'They're more made up than the clowns!'

'What's it all about?' they sang as a neon sign flashed 'The Real Thing' against a starless sky.

'What is real?' asked Jess as they got up to go.

'Have a nice day!' said a voice behind them.

The sky was bright with stars when they arrived at an African village. Outside a woman was grinding corn in a stone mill.

Inside, her five children lay sleeping. Miri offered to help grind the corn but the woman replied, 'No, my child. It has a rhythm and I am used to this work. The drought killed all the families but

ours – and today...' She paused and looked down. 'Today, my husband died. This is all the corn I have now. In the morning I will cook *sudsa* and we will eat our last meal.'

The twins were quiet for a while, listening to the slow, even grinding and seeing the faith in the woman's eyes. 'What do you need to live?' Miri asked, with tears on her cheeks.

'We have a saying, 'Every child brings its own bread'.'

'We can't leave them to die, Miri... but you know she'd never come...'

The Russian surgeon was proud to show the young travellers the new hospital. Above the operating table was a large mirror. 'This enables us to see the whole body without stretching over the patient,' she explained. The patient was drinking from a clear perspex cup. 'That's the pre-med, before the full anaesthetic. This man's body is riddled with cancer that we shall remove but it's very far gone as he didn't go to his doctor when he first felt unwell five years ago. If only he had ... modern medicine is marvellous...'

'Are we only a body, then?' Jesse wondered.

'I'm afraid you must leave, as the operation is starting.'

The Temple of Quest looked strange outside the angular concrete building. 'Off we go!'

'Isn't that lovely, sis?' shouted Jess, running towards the fountain to catch its spray. 'The sun has cast a rainbow over it – look! Let's throw three coins in the fountain and make our wish! And no telling!'

'We've still got two coins left – what about an icecream each?' Miri begged. 'One Paradiso and one Perfetto, please!' They sat in the sunshine, on the edge of the fountain bowl, madly trying to lick the icecream before it totally melted. 'Is there anything that lasts?' Miri asked.

'*Arriverderci, Roma!*' the ice-cream seller called.

'Have you noticed how no one ever answers our questions, Miri?'

Jess, where on earth are we now? We could be anywhere and there's no one in sight.'

The Temple of Quest hovered over a circle of five hills that surrounded a deep crater. They could make out the ruins of buildings and vehicles, and the remains of a bridge.

'I think a bomb's been dropped ... that's why there's no sign of life ... don't go any further.'

'I'm scared, Miri!'

'Hug me, Jess!'

Without speaking, they knew deep inside them that they must not look up. If they did, they would surely see the mushroom cloud – not the cup-shape they were seeking, but the cup-shape they were dreading... They flung their arms around each other's necks.

'Is this the end?'

***

Background and treatment
There are many legends about the Grail, the cup from which Jesus drank and in which drops of his blood were collected. About 1000 years go, there was a belief that if someone found the cup, asked it the right question and drank water from it, all the mysteries of life would be shown to them and they would live for ever. The Grail came in many forms and was sometimes even a stone: some thought about Jesus when they were searching for it and some thought of Mary. Often there would be a light or some sign above the Grail and the number five would somehow be important.

This is an adventure based on the Grail legends: a cup, bowl or similar – shaped object appears in each episode, as does a light or sign. Various supernatural hints are peppered throughout the text, such as the names for the icecreams and the two children's names, which are reminiscent of Mary and Jesus. This Grail story uses questions that young people might ask today.

Reflective questions
■ Nobody ever answered the twins' questions but did they get answers in other ways?

■ What is the Grail – that which you seek that is of ultimate value – in your life?

■ What questions do you ask in your quest for your 'Grail', on your journey through life?

■ What do you think are the most important questions for today's world?

Whoever Comes This Way
Strange how the grass never grows over that spot. All around, the grass is luscious in the rainy season, wispy in the drought. But there, just there, not a thing takes root. As if they'd learned the secret of the spot. no animals dare cross it. And travellers passing by stop in their tracks and step aside, as if gripped by an ancient taboo.

They say it's where a tortoise met her death. Plodding along, she heard a lion roar and saw it bound towards her from the jungle... She pulled her head inside her shell – and felt the creature pounce. Claws drawn, he rolled her over and she lay gasping on her back. And that was that, she knew: the hunt was up.

'Wait, please,' she cried. 'If I fight you, you will win. For you are big and I am small. You are strong and I am weak. You are fast and I am slow. But I have something else. Grant me this, I beg, one last request: a moment for myself before I die. Then you will surely have me for your prey.'

The lion loosed his grip and stood aside. It cost him nothing: he would take her soon. She leapt upon her feet and scratched the ground, pulling the grass out by its very roots. She kicked and scraped and dug and tore and raked. She saw the mound of earth she'd made and then she stopped.

'You are big and I am small. You are strong and I am weak. You are fast and I am slow. But I have something else. Whoever comes this way will see and know: I struggled to the end.'

Background and treatment
This African story is from the Zimbabwe region. Colonialism has shaped the self-concept of many peoples. Parallels with inequalities of power in the animal world serve to explore, in human affairs, layers of cultural and political expression, physical and economic exploitation, and social activism. The gender dimension in this version of the story offers the potential for an additional layer of interpretation.

Reflective questions

■ Why does the tortoise repeat her first words to the lion?

■ How can we understand the permanent effect on the land that the tortoise's actions seem to have?

■ Should the tortoise have attacked the lion and attempted to overpower him? Would that struggle have been nobler? Would submitting to the lion completely have been more dignified?

■ How and why does the tortoise struggle to the end?

A Match

One day God watched a match between the Yellows and the Purples.

For the first half, God put on the scarf, cap and emblems of the Yellow team, wore Yellow face paint and stood in the Yellow enclosure. The Purples scored three goals and each time the Yellow supporters just stood there silently, feeling very depressed. But God cheered really loudly, and leaped up and down. The Yellow supporters were really angry with God.

For the second half, God put on the scarf, cap and emblems of the Purple team, wore Purple face paint and stood in the Purple enclosure. The Yellows scored three goals and each time the Purple supporters just stood there silently, feeling very depressed. But God cheered really loudly, and leaped up and down. The Purple supporters were really angry with God.

At the station after the match, some Yellow supporters and some Purple supporters happened to meet. God was there too, with yellow and purple face paint, and purple and yellow scarves, caps and emblems. The Purple supporters and the Yellow supporters talked to each other about God: they thought God was really stupid or maybe even insane.

'What on earth,' they thought, 'could God be playing at?'

***

Background and treatment

Religions may come into contact with each other because they make competing truth claims but also because people use them when in dispute with one another over territory, resources, freedom and power. Participants in conflict frequently hold that 'God is on their side' in order to raise their own morale ad sense of righteousness rather than because they are genuinely religious. On the surface, sport provides a light-hearted metaphor for this opposition but there are serious undercurrents of hostility – both during and after the game of life.

This version of a modern tale of unknown origin offers a model for examining inter-religious and inter-ethnic relations on a wide scale in the world.

The metaphorical nature of the story is important to stress – and the story should be used with sensitivity and caution – because the personification of God is inimical to some religious and spiritual traditions. God's gender is unspecified.

Reflective questions

■ Why is God dressed like the supporters? Why might God support each side in turn?

■ In the station, why do the supporters focus their attention on God rather than each other or the game between them? What is the game now?

■ How is the match an image of the 'game of life'?

■ Why did the supporters think that God was 'really stupid or maybe even insane'?

■ What on earth *is* God playing at?

Five Journeys

An urgent call came to the great *Lama* of the north from the *Lama* of the south, asking for a wise and holy teacher to be sent to instruct young people in the south about the purpose of living. To everyone's astonishment the great Lama sent five teachers instead of one. Mysteriously he explained: 'We shall be fortunate if one of them gets to the *Lama* of the south.'

The group of five set off. They had been on the road for several days when a messenger came running up to them and cried: 'There is a terrible famine in our village, the rains and the crops have failed, the animals and people are starving, many have already died. Stay with us, we beg you, care for us, teach us knowledge of science and of nature.' – 'I would not be a Buddhist,' said one of the five teachers sent by the *Lama* of the north, 'if I did not stop here, and provide practical help for these suffering people.' The other four continued.

A few days later the four came to a city where some of the people on the streets exclaimed urgently to them: 'The governors of this city are uncaring and cruel. Stay with us here, we beg you, and help us to resist and to replace the people in power here, and to govern ourselves in justice and in peace.' – 'I would not be a Buddhist,' said one of the teachers sent by the *Lama* of the north, 'if I did not stop here, and join in resistance, politics and government.' The other three continued.

Some days later the three came to a town where there were frantic quarrels and arguments amongst members of different religious groups. 'Help us, we beg you,' said some of the people, 'to understand and to appreciate each other's festivals and customs. So that each person here feels rooted in their own tradition and history, but also feels respect for the traditions and stories of others.' – 'I would not be a Buddhist,' said one of the teachers sent by the *Lama* of the north, 'if I did not stop here, and help the people to find calm, and to live with each other in harmony and peace.' The other two continued.

A few days later the two came to a small settlement where all the people seemed marvellously happy. There were dances and games, paintings and music, embraces and laughter. There was ripening fruit on the trees, there were solid houses and homes, and everyone had challenging and valuable work. 'Settle with us here, we beg you,' said the people, 'set up home here, enjoy sexual love, nurture and cherish new human beings, join us here in building the future.' – 'I would not be a Buddhist,' said one of the teachers sent by the *Lama* of the north, 'if I did not stop and make my dwelling here, and enjoy the pleasures of everyday life.' The other continued.

Eventually the fifth teacher reached the *Lama* of the south, and began there the work which had been requested, and which was required, that of instructing young people about the purpose of living.

***

Background and treatment

This story is from the Tibetan Buddhist tradition, which places a strong emphasis on monastic education. A *lama* is a Tibetan Buddhist spiritual leader.

In the original version, four monks are distracted from their mission by worldly temptations. In this version, the four are distracted by something that is itself an element of the fifth teacher's message.

Reflective questions

■ What might the *Lama* have meant by 'We shall be fortunate...' Did he mean, fortunate if at least one gets through... or if only one gets through?

■ On reaching the south, what might the fifth teacher say about the other four teachers and their journeys?

■ Is the journey of the fifth teacher as important as – or more important than – the journeys of the other four?

■ It is often said that journeys are a metaphor for life: what might that mean?

■ What is 'the purpose of living' according to this story?

Nathan The Wise

by Gotthold Ephraim Lessing (1779), set in Jerusalem, 1192
Extract from Scene Six, in which Nathan and Saladin converse

Nathan

Once in the East there lived a man who owned a ring of unimaginable worth. It bore a jewel in which a thousand colours played and had the power to make the wearer loved by all people, and by God. No wonder that this man would never let it leave his finger or that he resolved that it should never leave his family. He bequeathed it to his favourite son and with it the instruction he in turn should pass it to his favourite son and that henceforth, ignoring all priority of birth, the favourite son should be the master of the house, by virtue of the power of the ring...

From favourite son to favourite son the ring passed down the ages till it came to a father who has three sons. All equally obedient, all equally attentive, all equally loved by their father. And so, according to which son pleased him most, at the end of a long day spent riding or talking, the embers dying in the grate, one by one he pledges the ring to each. Death approaches and now the father is dismayed. He cannot bear to think that two of his sons have trusted him and now must be denied, So he sends in secret for a jeweller and commissions him to make two copies, sparing neither cost nor effort till they are identical with the true ring. The jeweller obeys and when the rings are brought even the father can't tell which is the original and which the fakes. Joyfully he summons his sons one by one and gives to each his blessing and his ring. And so he dies...

That's it. I've reached the end. What happened next's predictable. The father's scarcely breathed his last before each brother comes with his ring and claims to be the master of the house. They haggle, they argue, they fight. In vain. No one can prove which is the true ring.

...

The sons argued. They brought the case before a judge. Each made a statement, swearing that he's received the ring directly from the father's hand. Which was true. That the father had promised him the ring at the end of a long day spent riding or talking, when the embers were dying etc. Which was also true. And each declared the father couldn't possibly have deceived him and that – much as he loved his brothers – it must be one of them to blame, and he would soon expose the traitor and then take his revenge.

The judge said this: 'This case will only be resolved if you can bring your father to the witness stand. Which you can't. Or if the true ring makes a statement. Which seems unlikely. Failing that, I must dismiss the case. But wait, I've heard the power of this ring is to make the wearer loved by god and by all people. Maybe that's your clue. The false rings could not do this. So think, which brother do the others love the most? Tell me. Or does each brother only love himself? If so then you're all deceived and all your rings are false. Perhaps the true one was mislaid, and the father had these three copies made as a replacement.'

'And so,' the judge went on, 'if what you want's a verdict, you must go elsewhere. But if you'll take advice, I'll tell you this: Accept the situation as it is. Each of you has a ring from your father, have faith that it's the true one. Maybe this was your father's plan, to end the tyranny of the single ring. It's clear he loved you all, and loved you equally: why should he disadvantage two by favouring one? You could do worse than follow his example, strive towards such unprejudiced affection in yourselves. Vie with each other to prove the power of your ring, through gentleness, tolerance, charity and a deep humility before the love of God. And if after a thousand thousand years the power of the ring still shines amongst your children's children's children, then I'll summon you again before this judgement seat. A wiser man than I will preside and he will give his verdict.'

***

Background and treatment

This play, written in post-Enlightenment Germany, was groundbreaking. It is thought to have derived from the friendship between Gotthold Ephraim Lessing, a Christian, and Moses Mendelssohn, a Jew – a friendship of the kind that would have been inconceivable even decades earlier. Indeed, it is likely that Lessing modelled the character of Nathan on Mendelssohn.

The play is set in Jerusalem in 1192 – the era of the Crusades, that is, of Christian-Muslim hostility of the extreme sort as each fought for domination of the city and the whole region. Caught in the middle is the small Jewish community. The play's two main characters are Saladin and Nathan, the former historical and the latter almost certainly fictitious. Saladin was the great Muslim leader Salah al-Din Yusuf who in 1187 recaptured Jerusalem for the Muslims, forbidding his soldiers to kill civilians, rob people or damage the city. Nathan, whose name means 'gift', is a merchant, respected by Christians, Muslims and Jew for his wealth and his wisdom.

The parable of the rings, which comprises the extract here, is occasioned by the Sultan asking the well-travelled and worldly-wise Nathan, 'Which code, which law, which faith have you found most enlightening?' Referring to Christianity, Islam and Judaism – the only three religions with which he would be likely to be familiar – he adds, 'Of these three only one can be the true religion.' Nathan in his reply – both directly and indirectly – begs to differ. Indeed, his parable of the rings suggests that there is no such thing as a true religion or, if there is, that we cannot be certain which it is. The parable and the play constitute a passionate plea for peace.

Reflective questions
■ How do we know what is true?
■ Are there truths that are only true for an individual or a community?
■ In what way might two opposites both be true?
■ If there is no absolute truth, is belief simply a matter of preference?
■ If an individual or a community believes that they have discovered or received the absolute truth, do they have a right to convince others of it? Do they have a duty to do this?
■ What should be our attitude towards people whose truths are different from ours?
■ How can we live with doubt about what is absolutely true?
■ Is there anything more important than knowing the truth?

■ Plays and Puzzles

This section of the book describes activities that can be used flexibly to support learning in several subjects, topics and themes. For most of them, you need to copy sheets to create sets of cards. A number employ role-play or simulation. Educationally they all engage pupils in:

- ■ clarifying their beliefs and values
- ■ handling paradox
- ■ coping with cognitive dissonance and what might be termed 'existential doubt'.

A practical point: when making sets of cards, put each set in a separate envelope or plastic wallet to keep them together and avoid the sets becoming muddled.

Religion is...

1. On page 00, there are ten vox pop snippets related to religion.

2. Make a copy of the sheet on card or paper, so that you have enough for one each per pair or small group in the class.

3. Cut up the copies so as to make sets of ten cards.

4. Consider also providing slips of paper to act as wild cards, on which pupils can write their own statements. Experience has shown that they seldom do! Nevertheless, the point of openness to alternatives is worth making.

5. Give out the sets of cards to the pairs or small groups.

6. Ask them to read each one aloud (but softly!) to one another, and to explain what they think it means.

7. Each individual should be given an opportunity to write their own statement about 'the meaning of life' on one of the wild cards.

8. Then have each pair or group choose nine cards (from the ten given plus any they have created) and rank them. Suggest to them the basis for selection and ranking, according to their needs or the demands of the curriculum. For example:

- ☐ 'True for members of religion X' (this provides a valuable summative exercise.)
- ☐ 'Relevant to event Y that we've been learning about'
- ☐ 'What you agree with'

9. Offer a diamond nine for ranking and write it on the board:

1

2 2

3 3 3

4 4

5

10. This ranking of the nine works best in five layers, because a strict 1-2-3-4-5-6-7-8-9 ranking needs too much refinement of thinking and there is inevitably some bunching around the middle range of relevance.

11. The members of any pair or group need to agree on both the discards and the ranking. This will involve a fair degree of negotiation – even haggling! For example, 'I'll move this one down if you move that one up...'

12. Then put two pairs or groups of pupils together, so that they can share their decisions and their reasons for them. You might ask them to reach consensus or at least to strive for it. Either way, they are called upon to use their skills of persuasion, based on reasoned argument.

13. You can consolidate the exercise by asking pupils to record their own results or you could organise a whole class perspective by presenting the findings, say, in a bar chart.

14. As an extension:

- ☐ Either ask individuals to choose **one** of the vox pop statements and write a story in which one of the characters speaks or otherwise expresses its sentiments
- ☐ Or ask the pair or group to choose **one** of the vox pop statements and enact a scenario in which one of the characters speaks or otherwise expresses its sentiments

You don't have to go to a religious building or anywhere like that to be religious.
You can pray anywhere you like.

Religions are all the same really; they just look different.

Someone I know meditates every day. I don't know how she does it but she's the kindest, most peaceful person I've ever met and I wonder if that's got anything to do with it.

There was a story in the papers about a man being picked on at work for his religion. You could tell what religion he was by the way he looked. It all got really nasty but he still didn't change. My mum says she wishes she could be strong like that about things. I just think he's stupid.

I don't see why there have to be so many different religions. Why can't they all agree? There's only one way to ride a bike so there should be only one way to be religious.

Our neighbour's child was very ill and the doctors couldn't do anything. Now they have these prayer meetings at home and they're hoping the child will get better that way. They've really changed.

My dad was taught that when you die all the good and bad things you've done get sorted out. So if you've been good, you go on to something better. But if you've been bad, you go on to something not very nice. Now he says all that does is stop people trying to make things better and just wait till they die. He says you have to take all the happiness you can when you're alive.'

Someone swatted a bee in class the other day – splat! – and it was dead. And I said, 'What was that bee born for – just to be squashed?' The teacher said, 'What were you born for, then?' and everyone laughed. I don't know, really. But I can't see why we should just get born and live and then die. There's got be more to it.

I can't see what good there is in religion. It seems to be behind so many wars and troubles in the world. If I had my way, I'd ban it.

Whenever I go to the countryside or I'm by the sea, it's really beautiful and I feel great inside. And I think: this world is all we've got and it's enough just to enjoy it.

RELIGIONS ARE SIMILAR IN THESE WAYS – AND MANY MORE

Element of religion	Buddhism	Christian	Hinduism	Islam	Judaism	Sikhism
being alone						
being together						
expressing identity in daily life						
marking important moments						
going to places that have special meaning						
telling stories and reading Holy Books						
expressing beliefs in symbols and rituals						
expressing ideas and feelings through arts						
expressing values in social action						
asking important questions, exploring what life means						

Religions are similar...

1. On page 80 there is a grid entitled 'Religion is similar in these ways – and many more'. Each of the six columns is concerned with a specific named religion or philosophical life stance.

   ☐ Consider substituting other religious traditions, philosophical life stances or ideologies to engage with as well as or instead of these.

2. Make a copy for each pupil. Because they need to fill it in, it is best to enlarge it to A3 size to allow for handwritten responses.

3. The exercise works well as a simple, fairly mechanistic means of reviewing the elements of the religions studied.

4. It appears to be focused on similarities. However, once completed, it is a useful tool for exploring diversity – or rather, diversity within unity.

'This World of Yours'

1. On page 82, there is a simple six-line dialogue. (Note that it appears twice on the sheet.)

2. Make enough copies so that each pair in the class (or trio if the class is uneven in size) has a set each. (In other words, halve the number of copies!)

3. Cut each sheet into twelve, making two sets of cards from each sheet.

4. Give a set of cards to each pair or trio.

5. Ask them to arrange the cards, by trial and error, so they make a continuous, coherent conversation. There seems to be an obvious sequence (as on the sheet) but alternatives are feasible.

6. This activity has several purposes, including that of developing pupils' linguistic skills and powers of reasoning. Key questions to ask are:

   ☐ Who is speaking to whom?

   ☐ What prompted the conversation to start?

   ☐ How might the conversation continue?

7. However, the greatest value is in considering the impact of the statement 'I have made you.' Given that the pupils will conclude that this is addressed to a person, group or the whole of humanity, further reflective questions can be asked, for example:

   ☐ What are the anger, hatred and misery about?

   ☐ What can be done about them?

   ☐ Who is 'you'?

   ☐ Why is 'you' made for this?

   ☐ What can 'you' do about it?

   ☐ Is the other speaker doing anything? Or is it enough to make 'you'?

This world of yours
is full of
anger, hatred and misery.

This world of yours
is full of
anger, hatred and misery.

I know.

I know.

Why don't you do
something about it?

Why don't you do
something about it?

I have done something
about it.

I have done something
about it.

What have you done?

What have you done?

I have made you.

I have made you.

The Bird and the Egg

This is not – or not necessarily – a visual version of 'Which came first – the chicken or the egg?' The humourous and thought-provoking picture story on page 84 was first seen on a poster in the Paris metro over 30 years ago, the original purpose long forgotten.

The Bird and the Egg raises all kinds of questions about the meaning of life, especially about the tension between the real and the ideal. It has been used successfully from the Foundation Stage to the Sixth Form. It can be used in two ways – the second of which (sequencing) is more engaging and therefore has more educational benefits.

As it is

1. Make a copy of the sheet for each pupil. Yellow paper or card is desirable.

2. Give them a few moments to 'read' the story quietly.

3. Then divide the class into groups of three.

4. Ask two of each group to tell the story to the other, in turn, with the third acting as an observer. (If the numbers are not divisible by three, allow for two observers in one or two groups.)

5. Ask the observers to note the differences between the two stories – particularly details that were supplied or ways in which the behaviour of the bird was interpreted.

6. The observers then report to the whole class on what transpired in their group.

7. Allow a few minutes for pupils to offer reflections on the process of interpretation in storytelling.

8. Most people are surprised by the last and also the penultimate image in the sequence. Ask the class why this is so surprising.

9. Now draw their attention to the image in the centre right of the sheet: the bird half in and half out of the egg, looking straight at you as it were, just after it has looked both ways. With young children, place this card on your forehead, to show that you are seeing the world according to this perspective.

10. Ask the class to imagine what the bird had just seen and what it might be thinking or feeling and intending to do – and why. Given that the bird eventually decides to return to the egg, ask them what they imagine made the prospect of life in the real world so daunting that it caused the bird to have a change of direction, a change of heart. They can respond through talk, writing or drawing – or a combination of all three – depending on their age and aptitude, as well as the time available. Their responses might be in 'bird' terms (e.g. no worms to eat, battery farming...) or in 'human' terms (e.g. wars... famine... injustice...)

11. Use these responses as an opportunity for them to clarify and crystallise their ideas of 'what's wrong with the world'.

12. But don't end there. Focus now on the first image (the whole, empty shell) in the top left hand corner of the sheet. With very young children, place this card on your forehead (as with step 9), to show that you are seeing the world according to this perspective.

13. Ask the pupils to speculate on what the bird might have imagined and hoped the world to be like before it emerged. You can use this as an opportunity for them to clarify and crystallise their ideals for life, humanity or the world. Again they can respond through talk, writing or drawing: their responses might be in 'bird' terms (e.g. juicy worms to eat... running around in the open air...) or in 'human' terms (e.g. peace between nations... love in families...)

14. Finally, ask them to explore the differences (physically, psychologically or philosophically) between the egg at the beginning and the egg at the end, and the differences that the whole experience might have made to the bird.

83

Sequencing

1. Copy the sheets to make one per pair or small group. Yellow paper or card is desirable.

2. Cut each copied sheet so that there are six picture cards per set.

3. Make two blank cards of about the same size and shape as the picture cards. These can be used as wild cards.

4. Arrange the class in pairs or small groups. Ask the pairs or groups to arrange the pictures so as to make a story. Allow them plenty of time to negotiate the sequence with one another. They can draw additional events in either or both of the wild cards.

5. Then ask them to create another story – or possibly more than one additional story, if time permits.

6. Ask each of the pairs or groups to tell the story (or stories) they created, using the six cards and any wild cards as visual aids.

7. Engage them in discussion about the idea that there are several versions of the story and explore with them what they feel about the fact that there seems to be no one right answer.

8. Then move to the sequence as shown opposite. Ask all the pairs to arrange their cards in this way. It may be that they have created this story, anyway.

9. Then proceed with the steps from 9 to 14 (on page 83).

10. Later the cards, with captions written by the pupils, can be mounted and displayed.

During discussion and when the pupils are viewing the display, encourage them to compare the various versions of the story and to avoid the temptation to decide which is the 'right' answer.

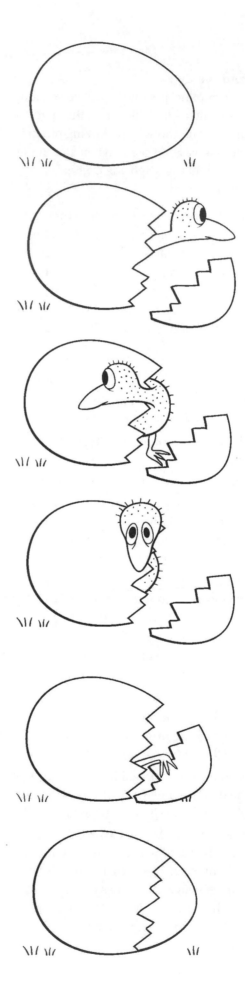

Top Secret

This activity is suitable for Years 7-13. It is designed to help secondary school students, through a specific experience, to realise that truth may be deceptive or elusive, and that there are many competing claims for the truth. **The instructions for the activity below may seem lengthy and complicated but it is in reality quite straightforward to conduct – and is remarkably effective.**

Essentially, it is an exploration of the fact that what is true may seem implausible or false, and that what seems implausible or false may be true. It is also an expression of the ways in which religious believers – and others – sometimes play their cards close to their chests.

The activity uses the 'Do not show this card to anyone else' sheets on pages 88-89. Note that there are two card sheets, which appear superficially the same. The four cards on the first sheet are the same; the four cards on the second sheet are the same; but the two sets of cards are slightly – yet significantly – different. For a convenient shorthand here, let's call the first set 'true' and the second set 'false':

- The 'true' cards start, 'Tell your group a story about something that happened to you'.

- The 'false' cards start, 'Tell your group a story about something that **you pretend** happened to you'.

The players work in groups of four (or five, if the numbers in the class are not exactly divisible by four). In each group, there is **one – and only one** – player with a 'false' card; all the others have 'true' cards. At the outset, the players do not know who has which – or even that there are differences in the text on the cards – and that is a key to the success of the activity.

Preparing for the activity

1. Use variously coloured paper or, preferably, card for copying the sheets (pages 88-89) to create the right number of cards for the class (see the chart on page 86).

2. The sheets of 'true' cards should be in different colours. The more the merrier but it doesn't matter which as long as the 'true' cards are in more than one colour.

3. The sheets of 'false' cards should be in the same colour so that you can see at a glance which member of each group has one. This should be a colour that is **not** used for any of the 'true' cards – **very** important. It's a good idea to use your favourite colour for the 'false' cards, so that you can remember which they are!

4. Ensure that you have made enough cards for the whole class. (It's wise to make a few extra to allow for any miscalculations and to cover any eventualities.) For example, see the chart on page 86.

5. Cut each sheet to make four cards.

6. Fold each card **almost** in half from top to bottom. That is, bring the bottom edge of the card up to the line at the **bottom** of 'DO NOT SHOW THIS CARD TO ANYONE', with the rest of the text hidden. Press down hard on the crease so that the card is unlikely to flap open. This means that if, when you come to give out the cards and players glance at them, they will believe that they all have essentially the same task.

7. Give thought to the composition of the groups, in particular to the one who is to have the 'false' card. This player needs to be someone who has a good imagination, and can take a joke and stand their ground.

Conducting the activity

1. Tell the class that they are going to tell stories to each other in groups, and that you are going to form the groups. If they are used to always forming their own groups according to personal choice and affiliation, tell them that there is a special reason why you need to form the groups this time.

Number in class	Number of groups	Numbers of cards needed
21	5 (4 groups of 4 plus 1 group of 5)	■ 16 'true' cards – assorted colours ■ 5 'false' cards – all the same colour
23	5 (2 groups of 4 plus 3 groups of 5)	■ 18 'true' cards – assorted colours ■ 5 'false' cards – all the same colour
24	6 (6 groups of 4)	■ 18 'true' cards – assorted colours ■ 6 'false' cards – all the same colour
27	5 (3 groups of 4 plus 3 groups of 5)	■ 22 'true' cards – assorted colours ■ 5 'false' cards – all the same colour
30	7 (5 groups of 4 plus 2 groups of 5)	■ 23 'true' cards – assorted colours ■ 7 'false' cards – all the same colour

2. Assign the groups and allow time for the chairs to be arranged in circles (with or without a table in the middle) and for the players to be seated so that they can all see the other members of their group.

3. Tell the whole class that you are going to give them a card with a story task on it and that they must not show their card to anyone else. **Secrecy at the outset is vital to this activity. Promise them that all will be revealed later – and keep that promise. This activity will only work with a class where you are confident that everyone can accept the discipline of not revealing their card until later.**

4. Hand out the cards to individuals, making sure that there is one – and **only one – 'false' card** in each group.

5. Give everyone a few minutes to read their card privately and to think about what they are going to say. There must be absolutely no conferring! Tell them that they will be telling a story to the others and may be asked questions about it. At the end of this preparation time, call 'time' – or even blow a whistle or ring a bell!

6. Now tell them that the storytelling is about to begin and that each player will tell their story for X minutes. ('X' will be a matter of your judgement: probably two to three minutes is about right.) There must be no interruptions during the storytelling.

7. After the first player in each group has told their story, call 'time' again and allow other players in the group to ask questions for up to one minute. These should only be questions of clarification.

8. Then call 'time' again. The next player in the group then tells their story for X minutes, followed by one minute of questioning.

9. And so on until all the players (including the 'false' one) have told their story and been questioned.

10. While all this is happening, circulate amongst the groups so that it appears that you know what people are saying. You'll find this interesting, anyway.

11. When everyone in each group has told their story and been quizzed about it, make an important announcement in a grave voice: 'I'm sorry to have to tell you that some

people in this class have not been telling the truth. In fact, there's one person in every group. I expect you to find out who it is.' Then allow a period of about five minutes for free questioning and speculation. The 'false' player may not be able to hold out and may spill the beans! That doesn't matter.

12. Some groups will inevitably discover earlier than others who the 'false' player is. You can ask them to come and stand quietly around a group that is still at the enquiry and speculation stage, and to goldfish bowl it – without interrupting or interfering.

13. Sometimes a group struggles to discover its 'false' player. This is actually a mark of the success of the activity but the pressure of time and perhaps the mounting frustration in the group may mean that it is sensible for you to ask the 'false' player to own up.

14. Be sure to allow time at the end of the lesson (at least fifteen minutes) for de-briefing and evaluation – and for the 'false' players, in particular, to be affirmed.

15. Discuss the lessons to be learned from this activity about knowing the truth. Certain questions have proved fruitful following this activity:

☐ Why can it sometimes so hard to find out what the truth is?

☐ Why might something false seem true?

☐ Why might something true seem false?

☐ If something is true on the surface, might it be false in a deeper sense?

☐ If something is false on the surface, might it be true in a deeper sense?

☐ Can something be true as an ideal even if it is not true in reality?

☐ Are there different kinds of truth? If so, are there different tests of truth?

☐ Are there some things that cannot be defined as true or false in any absolute sense?

☐ What has this to do with the ways in which we approach the claims to truth that are made by religious groups? In particular, what has it to do with competing truth claims made by different religious groups?

DO NOT SHOW THIS CARD TO ANYONE ELSE!

Tell your group about something that happened to you.

Describe what happened in a way that makes them **NOT** believe you.

You can leave out details and exaggerate other details. You can also say what you feel or think about your experience.

BUT you must **NOT** talk about anything that actually did not happen.

DO NOT SHOW THIS CARD TO ANYONE ELSE!

Tell your group about something that happened to you.

Describe what happened in a way that makes them **NOT** believe you.

You can leave out details and exaggerate other details. You can also say what you feel or think about your experience.

BUT you must **NOT** talk about anything that actually did not happen.

DO NOT SHOW THIS CARD TO ANYONE ELSE!

Tell your group about something that happened to you.

Describe what happened in a way that makes them **NOT** believe you.

You can leave out details and exaggerate other details. You can also say what you feel or think about your experience.

BUT you must **NOT** talk about anything that actually did not happen.

DO NOT SHOW THIS CARD TO ANYONE ELSE!

Tell your group about something that happened to you.

Describe what happened in a way that makes them **NOT** believe you.

You can leave out details and exaggerate other details. You can also say what you feel or think about your experience.

BUT you must **NOT** talk about anything that actually did not happen.

DO NOT SHOW THIS CARD TO ANYONE ELSE!

Tell your group a story about something that **YOU PRETEND** happened to you.

Describe what 'happened' **in a way that makes them believe you.**

It may have happened to someone else or be made up.

You can say what you think or feel about your 'experience'. But you must **NOT** describe something that actually happened to you.

DO NOT SHOW THIS CARD TO ANYONE ELSE!

Tell your group a story about something that **YOU PRETEND** happened to you.

Describe what 'happened' **in a way that makes them believe you.**

It may have happened to someone else or be made up.

You can say what you think or feel about your 'experience'. But you must **NOT** describe something that actually happened to you.

DO NOT SHOW THIS CARD TO ANYONE ELSE!

Tell your group a story about something that **YOU PRETEND** happened to you.

Describe what 'happened' **in a way that makes them believe you.**

It may have happened to someone else or be made up.

You can say what you think or feel about your 'experience'. But you must **NOT** describe something that actually happened to you.

DO NOT SHOW THIS CARD TO ANYONE ELSE!

Tell your group a story about something that **YOU PRETEND** happened to you.

Describe what 'happened' **in a way that makes them believe you.**

It may have happened to someone else or be made up.

You can say what you think or feel about your 'experience'. But you must **NOT** describe something that actually happened to you.

Party Politics

The four sheets on pages 93-96 are headed 'Party Politics'. They are role cards – but with a difference, as they are the resources for what is sometimes called in theatre-in-education (TIE) 'split briefs'. Here 'brief' is used to mean the information that someone has received and the stance they take as a result, as in a 'legal brief' or a 'design brief'. 'Split' implies not only different parts but also separate parts. The split brief technique is founded on two assumptions:

■ people in a given situation have different information about the situation and about the others involved in it

■ people in a given situation have different perspectives and personal agendas

Split briefs are particularly suited to ethical and spiritual issues that involve conflicting or diverging viewpoints. At many points in a split brief, conflict or divergence is spelled out directly, in as concrete terms as possible. Often the conflicting and diverging viewpoints derive from basic ideological differences between individuals and groups but sometimes they come through seeing things from a different perspective in a given situation – often because of different previous experiences.

Split briefs cards:

■ indicate that there is to be some kind of meeting, formal or informal, to talk about something: it might be a family over a meal at home, a group of friends at a club, a local community gathering, an international conference...

■ give some bald facts about the characters in the situation: their name and their formal connection to the others, their age or job if it is significant...

The issues in the Party Politics split brief are complex but the procedure is more straightforward than may at first appear. Nevertheless, it might be a good idea to create a split brief based on a situation that is less complex than in Party Politics – and start the class on that so that they get the hang of split briefs. Then proceed to Party Politics. You may

---

Party Politics is a play on words, as will become apparent:

■ there is a party at the home... and a political party member is a player...

■ there are references to local, national and international politics... and also family politics in the scenario itself...

This particular split brief involves complex issues centred on an emerging or enlarging religious and ethnic identities experienced by young people in Britain today, and the attendant family tensions. The national origins of the parent (character A) are not specified. The parent may be assumed to be of South Asian heritage but could be from virtually any country. When conducting the split brief, you will need to fine-tune this and to make it explicit to the class. You can do this in speech or by making a note on the split brief sheets – or both. Your choice will depend on the issues you wish to isolate for deep exploration and the relevance to the curriculum of the religious affiliation of the family in the split brief.

---

also go on to create other split briefs after Party Politics. If you want to create your own split brief – as well as or instead of this one – decide how many different viewpoints to isolate: two as a minimum and five as a maximum. Model the split briefs cards on the format of those on pages 93-96.

Preparing for the split brief

1. There are four players in Party Politics. Decide how many parallel scenarios you are going to run. It is particularly beneficial to have the class, in groups, working simultaneously. But there's no need to assign roles to everyone in the class at the outset. In fact, there is value in keeping some people out as observers, substitutes and interferers (details of these functions are below). For example, for a class of 28, consider six parallel scenarios (6 scenarios x 4 players = 24 students) and keep four out as 'extras'.

2. The same information appears at the **top** of each split briefs sheet:

☐ the names and some basic information about the four characters

☐ more detail about each of the four characters, their tastes, interests, feelings, thoughts, opinions, values and beliefs – their inner world – as well as their connections to one or more of the other players and particularly their attitude to the others in the situation and their perspective on the issue that will be discussed

3. At the **bottom** of each split brief sheet, there is further information about the named character and insight into what makes them tick.

4. Make copies of the split brief sheets: each character must have their own split brief sheet. Make a reference set for yourself, as well. Your job will be easier, as the split brief processes, if the photocopies are **colour-coded.** In other words, copy all the As on one colour, all the Bs on a second colour, and so on. This will help you see at a glance who's who in each group as you circulate between the groups.

5. Also consider writing the names of the roles on sticky labels for the characters to wear. For example:

'B: A's daughter, aged 14, born in Britain' or simply '**B**'

6. Give some thought to the formation of the groups, that is, who would play which role; and to the A-B-C-D combinations. Note that B is ideally female and C is ideally male; but A and D can be of either gender.

7. This can work in a conventional classroom but is better still in a hall or drama space.

Conducting the split brief

1. Introduce the activity as an exploration of family relationships on a weekday evening at home. But do **not** lead the witness by stressing that it is about contentious issues.

2. State the **religious affiliation** of the family (A, B and C) and the **national origin** of A and spouse.

3. Explain that they will be creating scenarios, without a script but with a brief on a role card. Explain the concept of 'brief' and check that it is understood.

4. Hand out all the A cards and get the A players into a huddle. Ditto with the Bs, Cs and Ds. In their huddles, the players should:

☐ read the general information about all the players, including themselves

☐ check between themselves that they understand what is involved

☐ agree some approaches to the family scene

The extras may observe these processes.

5. After huddling, create the family meeting groups, with one A, one B, one C and one D in each.

6. Stress that their split brief sheet should **not** be shown to anyone in the family meeting group. (Later – see 'Regrouping', below – there may be an opportunity for them to meet again with people of the same letter/colour.)

7. The play starts when all the participants are in a group and begin to discuss the issue in hand in role.

8. As the dialogue progresses, there are several ways in which you and any extra pupils might contribute and in which the drama of the situation can be heightened. You can use more than one in any split brief session. Here are five suggestions:

Swapping
Swap people performing the same role from one group to another. A player moving from one group to another has to remain in role but enter a situation where they are not exactly sure what has happened or been

said up to that point – just as in real life we often walk into a situation and have to make sense of what's going on.

Interfering

Ask someone from one group to give advice to the person playing the same role in another group, by whispering in their ear or passing them a note. They might stay with the new group for a while and reinforce what their co-player is saying or even take over. It means that their group will be without them for a while – just as when people drift in and out of meetings and gatherings in real life. Alternatively you could substitute one of your extras pupils as a participant – rather like substituting players in a sports match. Make sure that the extra has had an opportunity to read and absorb what is written on the relevant split brief card.

Regrouping

Intervene by suspending the dialogue and regrouping all those who are playing the same role: all the As together, all the Bs together... Give them the opportunity to huddle again, to confer, to exchange advice and perhaps agree on a new strategy in their respective groups. Then ask them to return to their own group.

Goldfish-bowling

This involves a whole group looking in on another group. It's particularly useful if dialogue in some groups is flagging but is sparkling in one particular group. It can be helpful to let the 'visiting' players stand or sit near the person playing the same role as them.

Pulling the cat out of the bag

Take on a role yourself – or ask one of the extras – as provider of additional information that might alter the content of the dialogue. Interrupt the dialogue by making an unexpected announcement, loudly enough for everyone in the room to hear, or else pass round a note. You might invent an item of local, national or international news, for example. The additional information should be decisive enough to affect the dynamics of the group and put a different complexion on the dialogue but not so dramatic that it makes it explode or come to an abrupt halt. You might plan what you are going to say or you might let the spirit move you.

9. It is highly unlikely that the conflicts will be resolved: they are much too profound and far-reaching for that. But there will have been a rich experience of exploration and insight.

10. Afterwards, consider a simple ritual for coming out of role, for example, asking each person to say who they acted and who they are. For example, 'I was C, A's son, aged 19, born in Britain. I am X.'

If you're making up your own split briefs, then – for the exercise to be effective – it's important to separate out the factors that are known to all participants from those that are known only to one participant. You may find it helpful to ask a colleague to check your cards after you've drafted them. After some experience of working with split briefs, students may be able to compose their own, too, but they also should have them checked by someone who's not going to participate.

PARTY POLITICS

Four characters

A   a parent, aged about 50, who came to Britain over 20 years ago

B   A's daughter, aged 14, born in Britain

C   A's son, aged 19, born in Britain

D   a local Councillor, aged 30+

A, B, C and D

When A and their spouse settled in Britain, they had a market stall where they sold cloth. Through hard work and determination, the business has now grown to a chain of fashion shops. All along they adopted a 'We're in Britain now' approach and did everything they could to fit into British society. They hate complaining and they don't even like being noticed. They always try to encourage their children to feel grateful to Britain for all the opportunities it offers them and for the good start in life that their schools have given them.

A has a spouse and there are also younger members of the family. B is in Year 9 and is choosing GCSE options. C has a job with good prospects in a computer firm. D is a committed political activist in the local community and became a local Councillor in the last election.

A

You're hard working, dedicated and energetic. You've suffered a lot of hardship and prejudice since you first arrived in Britain. But you've made a big effort to become a respected member of the community. You believe that things will improve if everyone pulls their weight, as you like to say, and they don't cause any trouble. Unfortunately your son, C, is a big disappointment to you and you think he has some wild ideas. Your daughter, B, is much more sensible and you hope to have her in the family business when she leaves school. You've just had her latest school report and the teachers say wonderful things about her. It's all very encouraging and you're both very proud.

> **You're planning a family gathering this evening, with a little treat to celebrate your daughter's achievements.**

PARTY POLITICS

Four characters

A   a parent, aged about 50, who came to Britain over 20 years ago

B   A's daughter, aged 14, born in Britain

C   A's son, aged 19, born in Britain

D   a local Councillor, aged 30+

A, B, C and D

When A and their spouse settled in Britain, they had a market stall where they sold cloth. Through hard work and determination, the business has now grown to a chain of fashion shops. All along they adopted a 'We're in Britain now' approach and did everything they could to fit into British society. They hate complaining and they don't even like being noticed. They always try to encourage their children to feel grateful to Britain for all the opportunities it offers them and for the good start in life that their schools have given them.

A has a spouse and there are also younger members of the family. B is in Year 9 and is choosing GCSE options. C has a job with good prospects in a computer firm. D is a committed political activist in the local community and became a local Councillor in the last election.

B

You're doing well at school and you're quite pleased with your report. You've always been encouraged by your tutor. She always wants to know more about your religion and it embarrasses you when you can't answer her questions. She's somehow helped you to find your faith identity that you thought you might have been losing, as your family got more involved in British society. Last year you went to a youth activity in your faith community centre and then started regular classes held there. You often cook and help out there at weekends and holidays, and you celebrate all the festivals. A couple of years ago you went to the country your family came from for a family occasion and it put you in touch with your roots. You hope to settle there when you are an adult. You know too well what your family are missing of their fine tradition. You can imagine that your move would disappoint and upset your parents but the clothes trade is definitely not for you. With the good school report you had today, you feel you'll be successful in your GCSE course and you'll be able to plan for the future with confidence. You're certain now and it's not fair to let your parents go on thinking that you'll join them in the business.

> **You want to tell your parents tonight what you're thinking of doing.**

PARTY POLITICS

Four characters

A   a parent, aged about 50, who came to Britain over 20 years ago

B   A's daughter, aged 14, born in Britain

C   A's son, aged 19, born in Britain

D   a local Councillor, aged 30+

A, B, C and D

When A and their spouse settled in Britain, they had a market stall where they sold cloth. Through hard work and determination, the business has now grown to a chain of fashion shops. All along they adopted a 'We're in Britain now' approach and did everything they could to fit into British society. They hate complaining and they don't even like being noticed. They always try to encourage their children to feel grateful to Britain for all the opportunities it offers them and for the good start in life that their schools have given them.

A has a spouse and there are also younger members of the family. B is in Year 9 and is choosing GCSE options. C has a job with good prospects in a computer firm. D is a committed political activist in the local community and became a local Councillor in the last election.

C

You're very unhappy in your job and you don't know why you went into computers in the first place. They're boring – and so are the people you work with. You don't seem to have anything in common with them and you can't stand their views. They can't stand yours, either. In fact, you've had quite a few hassles lately because they give you a hard time and call you names behind your back – or even to your face. You won't tolerate racism like that. Even when you were at school, you realised there was a lot in society that needed changing and far too many people put up with things that are really dreadful: racism, poverty, violence... Luckily, you've found a group of people at your faith community centre who think like you. One of the teachers there really knows their stuff about the Scriptures, what they said and how it applies today. It's given you a lot to think about. It's also helped you understand what's going on with your people in the country your parents came from and the situation they're in. When you went there a couple of years ago for a family celebration, you couldn't believe how dreadful their predicament is. You were very drawn to a particular group of activists that you met.

You feel you've go a lot to offer the family business and it needs to be more forward looking and more aggressive in its approach to marketing. You hope you could use some of the money you make to support the activist movement or groups that works for ethnic minorities in Britain. You think your parents have really sold out on their faith identity and on other minority groups. They're too concerned about their own security and status, and they don't listen to you.

> **You've invited a local Councillor to come over to your home tonight to discuss what can be done for minorities in your area.**

PARTY POLITICS

Four characters

A   a parent, aged about 50, who came to Britain over 20 years ago

B   A's daughter, aged 14, born in Britain

C   A's son, aged 19, born in Britain

D   a local Councillor, aged 30+

A, B, C and D

When A and their spouse settled in Britain, they had a market stall where they sold cloth. Through hard work and determination, the business has now grown to a chain of fashion shops. All along they adopted a 'We're in Britain now' approach and did everything they could to fit into British society. They hate complaining and they don't even like being noticed. They always try to encourage their children to feel grateful to Britain for all the opportunities it offers them and for the good start in life that their schools have given them.

A has a spouse and there are also younger members of the family. B is in Year 9 and is choosing GCSE options. C has a job with good prospects in a computer firm. D is a committed political activist in the local community and became a local Councillor in the last election.

D

You're keen to have a good reputation in the area as a really local person who cares about local things. You've got big political ambitions for yourself and your party. You made it quite clear where you and your party stood on racism and minority rights when you were campaigning before the last election. So you obviously think you were elected in order to put those ideas into practice. You've met C on various occasions. You think C will be a good ally.

> You're pleased that C asked you round this evening to discuss plans. You've been told that other members of his family are interested in what you have to offer – and they could be a key group in getting things going locally. You're determined to make a success of the meeting, to keep alive your ideas of a fairer society and to keep your party in the forefront of change.

The Peoples

This is a rich and fruitful activity – or rather series of related activities – for exploring an aspect of religion (specifically, wedding ceremonies). It enables participants to encounter through an intense experience the idea of diverging viewpoints and also the relationship between religion and culture. The content of this is especially well linked to gender, marriage and family themes. However, the content could be adjusted in order to serve other themes. Paradoxically perhaps, the tight structure enables pupils' creativity to emerge freely and constructively. There are some tangible as well as open-ended outcomes. This activity works well – with developmental adjustments – from Key Stage 1 to the Sixth Form.

The activity involves you as teacher as actor and you will have to alternate between your role as classroom manager and learning support on one hand and, on the other, as 'Chancellor' in the story that unfolds – unless you have one or more colleagues to take on the functions of classroom management and learning support.

It needs a great deal of time – ideally several hours – either as a series of lessons or as a half- or whole-day event during something like an Activities Week. There are important curricular links that you can develop between English, design and technology, art, music and drama, and religious education. However you distribute the available time, the stages outlined below are the same.

1. You will need to think of the class or large group as several small groups – each group as a certain people, for example, The People of the Forest, The People of the Mountains, The People of the Island, The People of the Countryside, The People of the Town... You can use imaginary places, if you wish, but not named real places. You'll need at least three groups for the activity to work well. At each stage, there's input from each People to the whole gathering so the more groups you have, the more time the whole activity will take.

2. If the space permits, it's best to arrange pupils on chairs in a horseshoe formation, with tables nearby, preferably behind them. Sit in the open gap in the horseshoe. If this doesn't work, arrange them in groups at tables, in a position to turn and face you at times.

3. Begin in role, without giving any clues as to what the whole activity is about. Be formal but warm. Greet each group 'People of the...' as you indicate with your hand who they are. Anticipate some giggling or shuffling at this point. Then, indicating the large space with your outstretched arm, say something, in an official tone, like:

   'Welcome to the Great Hall today and thank you for coming here at Royal Request. The Queen is sorry that she cannot be here to see you in person at the moment, to make her official announcement and to ask you to carry out three very important tasks but she has requested that I, her Chancellor, meet you. She hopes to arrive very soon and to see the fruits of your task. She knows that this is the first time in history that all her Peoples have gathered together and that adds to the importance of the occasion. None of you has ever met any of the other Peoples before and the Queen requests that you introduce yourselves, to talk about your journey here and to describe your life together in your land.'

4. At this point you might need to give each of the Peoples time (simultaneously, in parallel) to confer, to prepare what they are going to say about their journey, their environment and their lifestyle.

5. You'll need to allow at least three minutes for each People to report on their journey, their environment and lifestyle to the whole gathering. Sometimes, however, a member of each People can be asked to *ad lib* this, with others joining in and adding details. Sometimes a member of a People starts

spontaneously and the whole thing starts to flow. You can intervene or interrupt to elicit more detail, or encourage members of other Peoples to do so. The main purpose of this shared exposition is to enable each People to articulate their customs and any views of life that are embedded in them. Value judgements about Peoples' lifestyles, values and belief systems should not be made by members of other Peoples.

6. If there's a natural break here (such as the end of a lesson until next week or morning break during a whole-day activity), you can say that you will report what all the Peoples have said to the Queen and you're sure she will be very interested. If there isn't a break, you can pretend you have reported to the Queen by turning round and speaking or popping into the stock cupboard; or you can simply say that you will be reporting to her and you're sure she will be very interested.

7. You're now ready to make an announcement again in the Great Hall, as before. Say something like:

> 'The Queen wishes me to tell you that her daughter, the Princess, is soon to be married. And she invites all of her Peoples to the wedding. * But on one condition: each of her Peoples should bring to the wedding a gift for the Royal Couple, made yourselves from materials found where you live...'

> [* With older students, in particular, you can say something, if you like, about the Queen's personality or open government!]

8. If you have time and resources available, each People can then design and make a wedding gift. Otherwise give them time to discuss what they would make. With some classes, you might find it useful to discuss or suggest what sorts of things are conventionally given as wedding presents (useful or decorative items for the home) and what they might give to a couple who has everything.

9. When the gifts are ready or the ideas are agreed, reassemble the whole gathering in the Great Hall mode. Ask each People to present their gift or outline their gift idea, and to explain how it reflects the place where they live and the lives that they lead.

10. As before, go through the motions of reporting to the Queen before setting the second task. Say something like:

> 'After the wedding ceremony, there will be a Grand Banquet to which all the Queen's Peoples are invited. The Queen further requests that each of her Peoples prepares a piece of entertainment to be performed to all the guests. This could be a song, poem or dance from the place where her Peoples live.'

11. Again, discuss or suggest what might be appropriate entertainment for a wedding party, such as love songs or poems, funny or wise speeches. Pupils might be encouraged to draw, in general terms, from their own experiences of going to weddings or from any weddings they have seen in plays or films.

12. Then set the Peoples to work and, wherever possible, give them access to the resources they need, such as musical instruments or props or materials with which these can be improvised.

13. Repeat the 'show and tell' and 'reporting to the Queen' sequences, as with the wedding gift.

14. Then make another formal announcement in the Great Hall, something like:

> 'Most of all, the Queen hopes that her Peoples will participate in the wedding service itself. She requests each of her Peoples to create piece of liturgy or artefact for the service that comes from where they live. It could be words to be spoken or sung, such as a prayer, a hymn, a blessing or a wedding address, or a symbolic object that could be used in the ceremony.'

15. You could actually stipulate whether it is to be a piece of liturgy or an artefact or both. If it is to be an artefact, as with the wedding gift, you might make materials available or simply ask the Peoples to come up with an idea for an artefact. If the pupils have already had opportunities to explore wedding ceremonies, liturgy and artefacts, it may be enough for them to recall their essential features in order to undertake the task. If they haven't, you'll need to allow ample time now for discussing these in general terms or even break off into a study of a range of wedding rituals.

16. Pupils will find this third task very demanding but give them plenty of practical and moral support. It's the most important of the three tasks and the one to which the other two have been leading.

17. Repeat the 'show and tell' exercise as with the wedding gift and the piece of entertainment. This time, however, as you go to report to the Queen and find that she is unavailable, there just happens to be a piece of paper on the floor – and you just pick it up. Have a note prepared – on a large sheet of paper, preferably in a conspicuous colour – along these lines:

> *Dear Queen,*
> *I have gone away.*
> *I do not want to marry him.*
> *Love from your daughter,*
> *The Princess*

18. At this point, the prescribed structure breaks down and there is a lot that will need to be played by ear. You have a lot of scope and choice but it's essential that the Peoples get to find out what the note says. You can simply read it out or pretend that you can't read the language and ask a member of one of the Peoples to read it or debate whether you should read someone else's post. Invariably, everyone wants to know what it says. Their reactions might be strong and you have to think on your feet. You can then, still in the Chancellor role, ask the Peoples to decide what should be done:

they might need some guided discovery! They might decide to:

a. have the party anyway since they've gone to a lot of trouble

b. demand to see the Queen and let her say what's to happen: you can either insist that she's unavailable or else produce someone to be the Queen or else ask them to rehearse what they would say to the Queen if she appeared in the Great Hall then and there. You can, for example, say, 'I am the Queen's Chancellor and I can't possibly summon her here without knowing what you're going to say.' You could elect someone to play the part of the Queen and to listen to what the Peoples have to say. They might be aggressive, of course, or cross that she seems to have been forcing her daughter into a wedding against her will. They might invent all kinds of unsavoury facts about the intended spouse!

c. go looking for the Princess to force or persuade her to come to the wedding; or, out of curiosity, to find out why she went away and doesn't want to marry her suitor; or, out of concern, to see why she is troubled and what they can do to help. As with b, above, if they want to see the Princess, you can produce her or else ask them to rehearse what they would say if they found her. Ideas about arranged and assisted marriages, about expectations of marriage and of the roles of partners are likely to emerge and may need sensitive handling. It might transpire that she has had a quarrel with her intended spouse or that they have different of views on religion or politics or their plans for the wedding, their future life together, the raising of children. It might help, therefore, to produce the intended spouse in the rehearsal to see what he has to say. All these possibilities are useful discussion points and highly relevant to the issue of divergent viewpoints, the nature of religion and the relationship between religion and culture. You, as Chancellor, can encourage the Peoples to act as go-betweens: they could ferry messages between the couple, or offer them advice or practical help. The possibilities are endless. (By the way, most Peoples are likely to opt for a version of this c scenario.)

d. do something that no other group has done yet – in which case, you're on your own: *ad lib* away!

19. Although this story-making activity is in the genre of fairy tale, it may not necessarily have a happy ending: the couple may not necessarily live happily ever after and it does not necessarily follow that a good time was had by all at the party. If it does, however, it may be a good case for staging the wedding that has been envisaged, using all the liturgy and artefacts created, throwing the party as planned and presenting the gifts. Another class – or other members of the school community – might be invited to observe. It makes a very effective assembly.

20. Afterwards, whatever the choice made and whatever story unfolds, it is important from an educational point of view for the pupils – out of role – to discuss what happened and the processes involved, and to evaluate what they gained from it.

Two by Two

Two by Two is a talk-based activity and can be very lively indeed. It seems complicated but is easier to manage than it is to explain how to manage. Mechanically, it's quite straightforward. It may be suitable for Key Stage 3 but is likely to be more profitable with students at Key Stage 4 or in the Sixth Form. It also has an application within a professional development programme.

Two by Two involves the participants making a series of deceptively simple decisions between numbers in the abstract in order, they are told, to 'maximise their score'. The complexity lies in the values underlying these numerical choices, values to be teased out afterwards. It has been proven to be invaluable in an exploration of conflict, complexity and controversy.

Two by Two is based on the interaction of responses between two groups, each of which has a simple choice to make between two alternatives without knowing the choice made by the other group until it had made its own. The energy appears to reside only in the interaction of responses between the two groups. But there is also energy in the interaction within each group as decisions to be made are discussed: this increases as the activity progresses and the results of earlier decisions become apparent. Some individuals also experience an energy within themselves as they ponder the dilemmas involved and their role within their group.

It's a **non-zero-sum** activity to engage individuals and groups in responding to a particular experience of conflict, and to explore concepts such as cooperation and competition, harmony and conflict, negotiation and compromise, risk and trust, guilt and forgiveness, and the nature of success. Ultimately insights emerge about 'the meaning of life'. Sometimes groups realise that the only way to win is for both groups to win – but keep that very much under wraps, at least until after the activity is over.

> Debriefing after the activity is essential to its effectiveness, as well as to ongoing relationships between participants. Adequate time must be allowed for it.

This activity is devoid of specific content or, rather, its content is abstractly arithmetical. This means that both the product and the process of the activity can be applied to any and every issue of conflict. It has been used from Key Stage 2 to adult groups. It's wonderful for staff team-building sessions and in the context of professional development on conflict management. Participants need to have a grasp of the principle of simple arithmetic – multiplication and the concept of negative numbers. Otherwise they will not understand their scores and how to proceed further. You, the teacher, need to multiply small numbers, including negative ones, and make simple additions.

Preparing for the activity

1. Two by Two is suitable for a class or group of up to about 30 members (to be divided into two groups).

2. This activity ideally needs $1^1/_2$ hours to run, including the period of 20-30 minutes of shared reflection afterwards. If necessary, however, you can shorten the time for play by omitting some of the stages (see chart for recording decisions, on page 106.) If only one hour is available, allow a maximum of 40 minutes for play; 20 minutes of discussion is the minimum.

3. You will need two rooms – one for each group – in close proximity, as you need to go back and forth between them. Each room must have a door so that the groups can have discussions in private.

4. It is also preferable to have an additional neutral space for the briefing beforehand and the debriefing afterwards. If a third space is not available, you can use the two group rooms – ideally one before and the other afterwards, so that there is no suspicion of bias. There might also be consultations between individual representatives from each group. These can take place in the neutral third space, if you have one; otherwise somewhere like a corridor. It must be out of earshot of the two groups.

5. For **each group**, make a copy of the interplay grid (on page 105). This should be on a sheet of paper or card that is at least A3 in size, preferably A1.
   - ☐ Use black for the lines of the grid.
   - ☐ Use a second (dark) colour for '1', 'X', 'Y' and the numbers in the top left corners of the squares: '+5', '+3', '-5' and '-3'.
   - ☐ Use a third (dark) colour for '2', 'A', 'B' and the numbers in the bottom right corners of the squares: '-5', '+3', '-3' and '+5'.

   You may also find it useful to have a small (e.g. A4) version of this grid to keep with you for reference, as you move back and forth between the groups.

6. For **each group**, make a copy of the chart for recording decisions (on page 106). This should be on a sheet of paper or card that is at least A3 in size.
   - ☐ Use black for the lines on the chart and the words 'DECISION', 'SCORE THIS STAGE', 'RUNNING SCORE', 'Stage 1' etc. and 'CONSULTATION?'
   - ☐ Use the second colour (used for the grid) for 'Group 1'.
   - ☐ Use the third colour (used for the grid) for 'Group 2'.

   You **definitely need** a small (e.g. A4) version of this chart to keep with you to record decisions as they are made and to convey one group's decisions to the other.

7. In each room, make it possible to display one copy of each chart on the wall or prop them up on a chair – but don't do that yet. Arrange chairs in a near-circle, so that both charts will be visible to all participants.

8. Give some thought in advance to the best way of dividing the class into two groups of about the same size. Aim for two groups that seem balanced in terms of strong personalities, as well as formal leaders. You may appoint a procedural chair in each.

9. Consider the advantages of a non-participatory observer in each group. Their observations during the reflection period

will be invaluable. The observer must be capable of taking notes during the play and of not speaking. This might be a teaching assistant in a primary school or a member of the class in a secondary school. Do not use as an observer anyone who might be perceived as authoritative or intimidating, as paranoia sometimes develops when groups feel they are losing and they sometimes suspect the observer of invisibly affecting results. For example, in a professional development session, the headteacher should not be an observer.

10. You will need to have during the play:
    - ☐ a watch
    - ☐ a black marker pen in each room for recording decisions and scores on the chart in each room
    - ☐ a pen for recording decisions on your small recording chart
    - ☐ if engaging observers, pens and paper for them to make notes

Briefing the class/group for the activity

1. If you are using observers, brief them before the group briefing on their roles and responsibilities. They are to:
    - ☐ watch and listen
    - ☐ **not** speak or communicate non-verbally with members of the group
    - ☐ make a note of reasons given for group decisions and any values underlying those decisions that are made explicit
    - ☐ be prepared to **report non-judgementally** afterwards on the decision-making process, **without naming individuals**

2. Begin with a briefing to the class or whole group together, in the neutral space, if you have one. If time is tight in the session in which you plan to run the activity, you can conduct the briefing beforehand but do not announce the membership of the groups at this stage.

3. Be transparent about the balance and equality of the two groups by having both sets of charts available so that all can see that they are the same.

4. You can use one set of charts to make it clear what you mean, as you describe the activity.

5. Explain that Two by Two is a game (you can use that word!) played by two groups in separate rooms.

6. State clearly that the **purpose** of the game is for each group to maximise its scores. You could say, 'Your aim in your group is to get the highest score that you can. You will have several go's at this.'

7. Showing the interplay grid, say something like: 'One group will be '1' and the other will be '2'. Group 1 chooses between 'X' and 'Y', and Group 2 chooses between 'A' and 'B'. When you choose, you don't know what the other group is choosing straight away. When the two choices are put together, the two groups get their scores.'

8. Then give a couple of examples, along one or more of these lines, depending on how much explanation you feel that the class or group needs (because it's a two-by-two perm, there are only four possibilities):
    - ☐ If Group 1 chooses **X** and Group 2 chooses **A**, then it's the top left square, so group 1 gets +5 and group 2 gets-5.
    - ☐ If Group 2 chooses **A** and Group 1 chooses **Y**, then it's the top right square, so Group 2 gets +3 and Group 1 +3.
    - ☐ If Group 1 chooses **X** and Group 2 chooses **B**, then it's the bottom left square, so Group 1 gets -3 and Group 2 gets -3.
    - ☐ If Group 2 chooses **B** and Group 1 chooses **Y**, then it's the bottom right square, so Group 2 gets +5 and Group 1 gets -5.

9. Explain that you will come in and collect the two groups' decisions one at a time, work out their scores and record them on the chart. Point to one of the recording charts and show the spaces for the letter decisions, for scores at each stage and for the running total. (At the first stage, the SCORE THIS STAGE and the RUNNING SCORE are the same.)

10. Point out that there are opportunities built in for consultation, if both groups agree to consult. This will involve one individual from each group: it need not be the same individual each time. These ambassadors can negotiate commitments to make certain decisions for future stages.

11. Now announce the memberships of the groups and send them to their respective rooms, with their two charts to put up. Say that you will arrive 'in a moment' to hear their first decision which they must all be agreed on. They can elect a leader to chair their discussions, if they feel the need. Alternatively, you can appoint a procedural chair in each group.

Conducting the activity

This is a series of pointers rather than a set of chronological steps.

1. During the activity, your role is to collect decisions, compute the scores and record them.

2. You also have a major task in keeping the decision-making processes running along smoothly so keep a close eye on the time.

3. Be very formal – officious, even – in your demeanour. You must be impartial and seen to be impartial. Do not be drawn into discussions about the decisions to be made and do not comment on them.

4. It will be very tempting to linger with a group if their discussion interests you – and the discussions can be very interesting indeed. Resist that temptation! You don't have time and you run the risk of being seen as partisan.

5. It can happen that one group has made a decision but the other has not, which causes that stage to be delayed. This can create frustration and a sense of unfairness. Try – though admittedly it is difficult – to allow both groups the same amount of time. Certainly collect the decisions alternately. In other words:

   ☐ Collect the decision from Group 1 and record the letter on their big chart – but **most importantly on your small one.**

   ☐ Visit Group 2 and collect their decision. Inform them of Group 1's decision (always a good idea to read it from your chart as it ensures accuracy and conveys a sense of officialdom). Record the decisions on their chart and compute the SCORE THIS STAGE and the RUNNING SCORE. Record this on their chart. **Also write all this on your small recording chart.**

   ☐ Tell Group 2 to start making their second decision that you will be 'back in a moment' to get it.

   ☐ Return to Group 1 and inform them of Group 2's first decision. Complete their recording chart (as above).

   ☐ Next time, repeat the process in reverse, that is, first collect Group 2's decision. This will, over the stages, more or less even out the amount of time that the two groups have to make their decision. It will also dispel any suspicion that you are taking sides with the group that announces it decision second.

   ☐ Carry on like this, zigzagging evenly between the two groups.

6. The first decision needs a little extra time because it involves the participants in coming to terms with the arithmetic. They may also be engaged in deciding whether they need a chair and, if so, who it should be – unless you have settled this issue in advance.

7. The next few decisions often come thick and fast as the groups settle on a strategy. Mostly they are initially aiming for +5, which is ultimately a loser. As they usually come to realise this, they need longer to consider alternatives.

8. There is an opportunity for consultation at various points if both sides wish. If they do, give them a moment to decide what their bargaining terms are and who will represent them. If there are subsequent consultations, the groups may choose a different representative, as well as different bargaining terms.

103

9. The groups are not bound by the terms they agreed in the consultation. In fact, one group may use the trust engendered in the consultation to double-cross the other. There are cases of double-double-crossing, too! In subsequent consultations, groups sometimes try to negotiate a pay-back after a double-crossing. Some groups play clean, some dirty and some clean only if the other plays clean...

10. At the end of Stage 10, point out to the groups that the stakes are raised for Stages 11 and 12 as the scores are doubled. Likewise, at the end of Stage 12, the trebling of scores for the final stage, Stage 13.

Reflecting on the activity

This is a series of general pointers, born of experience. But not all the outcomes can be anticipated and much needs to be *ad libbed*.

1. When the game is over, you may wish to consider allowing the groups a moment to reflect on the process. You might even ask them to prepare a statement to make to the whole of the other group when they reconvene.

2. Draw the two groups together. If you used a third neutral space for the briefing, that is the place for the debriefing, too. If you used one of the group rooms for the briefing, use the other for the debriefing. The two groups are not likely to intermingle and may sit apart with considerable distance between them. There may be great tension or even anger.

3. If the groups have a statement to make, this is a good starting point.

4. If you engaged observers, allow time for them to report on what they reflected.

5. In the presentations and discussions that follow, the language of winning and losing is likely to be employed. That is, the group that achieved the highest score – or anyway, the least low score! – will deem itself to be the winner. Almost all groups end with a negative score or at least a very low positive score. It is useful to point out that the target

was for each group to maximise its score – and not necessarily beat the other group. You can explain that:

☐ If one group scored +5 each time, it would achieve a total score of +105, including the doubles and treble. But it is **impossible** for both groups to get +5.

☐ Yet it is possible for both groups to get +3 each time. That would yield a score of +51, including the doubles and treble. It is highly improbable that either group achieved anything remotely resembling that score!

6. In other words, the groups may have seen Two by Two as a zero-sum or win-lose game in which they succeed in relation to the other group's failure. In fact, it is a win-win game where the biggest winning for both groups (+3 and +3 at each stage) comes from a little losing.

7. It is worthwhile to reflect on the various levels of conflict that might have been experienced during the decision-making process:

☐ between groups

☐ within each group

☐ within an individual

8. Key questions to pose are:

☐ How could Two by Two have been played differently so that both groups achieved their goals?

☐ What situations in life are similar to Two by Two?

☐ There are lessons to be learned from Two by Two – what are they?

☐ What does winning mean?

	1	
	×	**y**
A	+5 ⋅⋅⋅ -5	+3 ⋅⋅⋅ +3
2		
B	-3 ⋅⋅⋅ -3	-5 ⋅⋅⋅ +5

	DECISION		SCORE THIS STAGE		RUNNING SCORE	
	Group 1	Group 2	Group 1	Group 2	Group 1	Group 2
Stage 1						
Stage 2						
Stage 3						
Stage 4						
Stage 5						
Stage 6						

CONSULTATION?

Stage 7						
Stage 8						
Stage 9						
Stage 10						

CONSULTATION?

Stage 11 scores x 2						
Stage 12 scores x 2						

CONSULTATION?

Stage 13 scores x 3						

■ Reporting on Reporting

Not a day passes without reference in the media to religious and cultural groups. Indeed, most days there are several such newspaper articles and items on radio and television news programmes. They almost invariably portray religious and cultural groups in a negative light – typically as either 'exotic' or as narrow, closed and backward. Very seldom are they presented as genuinely attractive or normal: they are otherised. In particular, there is a heavy focus on conflict: within a group; between groups; and between the ethos of the group and 'the British way of life'. The latter is hard to identify and it is fallacious to suggest that it is monolithic. Nevertheless the media assume that their readers, listeners and viewers will know what is meant and indeed believe that it exists. This assumption further otherises religious and cultural groups.

It is known that children and young people are not prone to reading newspapers, listening to radio news broadcasts or watching television news programmes. Nevertheless, they are likely to pick up – perhaps uncritically – the attitudes and values of older people who do. In time, children and young people are statistically likely to read, listen to or view the news for themselves: learning to read and decode the media can make a potent contribution to education in literature and the humanities including religious education, especially as they interface with citizenship education. Therefore, before children and young people become regular media consumers, it makes sense for them to have structured opportunities for exploring and, where necessary, deconstructing the media; and particularly the experience of modelling by the teacher. This makes it learning for life.

The material in this section of *What do we tell the children?* is free of prescribed content: the focus is on learning skills. In particular, it stimulates pupils' ability to identify a 'mistake' in the media, reflect upon it and make an informed response. Clearly the skills of critical enquiry are highly sophisticated and developing them is particularly demanding for you as teacher.

This resource scaffolds the process with suggested steps and accompanying templates for pupils to report on the reporting. It consists of generic guidance for them; suggested activities for you to facilitate; and templates for use with any media content.

One of the greatest challenges for us as teachers is managing – ethically and educationally – the anger and distress that many pupils feel when they encounter and explore media portrayals of religious and cultural groups, as well as of other vulnerable peoples.

Two sets of separated but related resources have been created:

■ Media Watch
■ F-A-I-R-N-E-W-S

This resource can be used flexibly. However, there is a summary of suggested steps on page 115.

A starting point

It is advisable begin with an exploration of what constitutes fair reporting. This is most effective if it is initially removed from the context of local, national or international reporting of an incident involving one ore more religious or ethnic groups. Rather it should relate to a more accessible event, such as a hypothetical but typical school incident that involves differing viewpoints and different understandings of what actually happened. This is appropriate because reporting of events related to religious and ethnic groups almost invariably focuses on matters of conflict.

In considering the everyday incident, pupils are likely to propose, for example, the idea that there are 'two sides of the story'; that it is wrong to 'pick on' some of the players; and that 'who started it' is of some but not absolute relevance. They should be encouraged to share their understanding of the concept of fairness and to attempt to provide a checklist – however tentative – of criteria that might be used in judging the fairness of the way that similar incidents are recounted, recorded and reported.

If individual, group or whole-class checklists are created, make a secure record of them for future use.

Media Watch
Guidance and differentiated templates are provided for a series of opportunities to examine media reporting of religious and cultural groups – specifically the conducting of investigations:

- a two-page guidance paper for pupils, on pages 109-110
  - ☐ Pupils need a copy of this for their reference and may need to use it more than once.
- one version of a two-page template for the results of the investigation, on pages 111-112
  - ☐ This version has **graphic triggers** (matched to the guidance paper) and relatively little space for written responses. The structure mirrors that of the guidance paper. In the 'summary' box, pupils can choose to summarise in words or by means of a sketch. This version is especially appropriate at Key Stage 3 and for older students who need this kind of support, especially when it is their first experience of using this template for reporting on reporting.
- another version of a two-page template for the results of the investigation, on pages 113-114
  - ☐ This version has no graphic triggers but a **substantial space for written responses**. The structure mirrors that of the guidance paper. This version is especially appropriate at Key Stage 4 and for younger pupils who need this kind of challenge or have had successful experience using the version with graphic triggers.

The most effective way to manage the process is by first modelling an investigation for the class or group involved, so that they benefit from an **informed response** to the media's treatment of an event involving a religious or cultural group.

The sample you choose need not necessarily be recent but should be one in which the issues are relatively clear and unequivocal. The sample can be from any of the four media on the guidance: print, radio, television or the Internet. It is vital that all the pupils have access to your chosen sample by:

- either reading a copy of the printed text
- or listening to a recording of the radio news
- or watching a recording of the television news item
- or visiting the website

The next step is for pupils to conduct an investigation on their own, in pairs or possibly in small groups. It is advisable for them – at least for their first reporting on reporting experience – to be **given** a sample of a media report, because their search can result in an unproductive use of time and can become very dispiriting. It also means that the pupils are not disadvantaged if they don't have access to daily newspapers, the radio, television or the Internet at home. If a personal choice is preferable – particularly at Key Stage 4 – time the assignment so that pupils can use resources and facilities at school or a public library.

After one or more Media Watch investigations, pupils can then refine their understanding of what makes reporting fair – and the checklists of criteria that were devised earlier can be amended.

Media Watch

Look out for media reports of things happening in or to religious or cultural groups.
You could find them in:

a newspaper or magazine article

a television programme or news broadcast

an Internet website

a radio programme or news broadcast

Whatever you watch, hear or read, examine it closely. Then make your report.

YOUR MEDIA WATCH REPORT

Identity

Give your name, tutor group and the date you made your report.

Source

- For a **newspaper or magazine**, give its name, the title of the article and the date it was published.

- For a **television or radio** programme or news broadcast, state the channel or station, the title of the programme and the date it was broadcast.

- For an **Internet website**, give its address, the name of the group that hosts it and the date the page appeared.

Subject

In a few words, say what the article, programme or web page was about (for example, a religious festival, rally or demonstration, terrorist act, war, peace talks...)

Summary

Either sum up in your own words what the article, programme, news broadcast or web page said on this subject. This can be a list of numbered or lettered points.

Or sketch an image from the article, programme, news broadcast or web page.

Questions

What did the article, programme, news broadcast or web page make you wonder about? Did it leave any questions in your mind?

Omissions (things that have been left out)

What else do you need to know about the subject that the article, programme, news broadcast or web page did NOT cover?

Images of. . .

What kinds of image of the religious or cultural group do you think the article, programme, news broadcast or web page showed? Were these images positive or negative? Say why.

positive ('good')?   negative ('bad')?

Personal feelings and responses

What did the article, programme, news broadcast or web page make you feel? Say why. Perhaps you have 'mixed feelings'.

Media Watch

My Media Watch Report

Identity

Name _____

Tutor group _____ Date _____

Source

_____

_____

_____

_____

Subject

_____

_____

_____

Summary

writing
(numbered
points)
or
drawing
(sketch or
sketches)

Questions

Omissions

Images of. . .

Personal feelings
and responses

Media Watch

My Media Watch Report

Identity

Name _____

Tutor group _____ Date _____

Source

_____

_____

Subject

_____

_____

_____

Summary

_____

_____

_____

_____

_____

_____

_____

Questions

_____

_____

_____

_____

Omissions

_____

_____

_____

Images of. . .

_____

_____

_____

_____

Personal feelings and responses

_____

_____

_____

_____

_____

F-A-I-R-N-E-W-S: an approach to examining fairness in the media

Following Media Watch investigations and reflections, pupils might be introduced to the 'F-A-I-R-N-E-W-S' criteria, which are set out on pages 116-117. It may be helpful for them to compare this list with the one they devised, to spot similarities and differences, and to refine further or reinforce their thinking. This is most appropriate for Key Stage 4 and for some at Key Stage 3. 'F-A-I-R-N-E-W-S' is very comprehensive and has the value of being an effective aide-memoire but the extent to which pupils benefit from the earlier process of their own discoveries and discussions cannot be over-estimated.

Each of the eight 'F-A-I-R-N-E-W-S' criteria ends with a short set of questions, the last of which in each case is 'What can we do about...?' This urges pupils to consider practical ways in which the responsibility to seek truth and pursue justice might be exercised. No guidance is provided on how to respond in a concrete way to unfair reporting, such as by addressing complaints to the media. Yet pupils may identify such a solution, if only in theory.

On pages 118-119, there is a 'F-A-I-R-N-E-W-S' template for pupils to use. This follows the structure of the 'F-A-I-R-N-E-W-S' criteria on pages 116-117.

Point out to pupils that when they are applying the 'F-A-I-R-N-E-W-S' test to a news item, they may not find evidence to test all eight criteria. Likewise, they do not necessarily need to search in the order of the sequence of the acronym: sometimes one of the criteria jumps off the page or screams from the television – and that is a good place for them to start.

There will be some individuals and groups who do not need Media Watch and can begin with F-A-I-R-N-E-W-S. It is a matter of your assessment of their aptitudes and your professional judgement as to what is most appropriate.

At this stage, pupils undertake an investigation of a current news item. They will have discussed and explored some criteria against which to judge the extent to which a report of an everyday event or a news item is fair reporting. Now is the moment of reckoning: how far have they understood the principles of fair reporting? which skills have they developed in detecting the features of fair and unfair reporting? This is therefore rightly a finale. It works both as learning experience and also, if you wish, as a means of assessment.

This guidance takes pupils step-by-step through the process of an initial analysis of a news report by, for example, differentiating between the subjective and the objective. As such it makes this complex process manageable. It also has the advantage of acknowledging the importance of personal feelings and responses, at least at the initial stages. It encourages pupils not to follow their hunches but rather to **follow through** on their hunches.

A summary of possible steps in teaching Reporting on Reporting

- Opening discussions on what makes for fair reporting

- Creation of draft checklists of criteria

- 'Media Watch' on a sample, modelled by you the teacher using one of the templates

- Pupils conducting one or more Media Watch investigations, using one of the templates

- Refinement of checklists of criteria

Possible end here... or continue...

Possible beginning here...

- Introduction to F-A-I-R-N-E-W-S *aide-memoire*

- Comparison between F-A-I-R-N-E-W-S *aide-memoire* and checklists of criteria

- F-A-I-R-N-E-W-S on a sample, modelled by you the teacher, using the template

- Pupils conducting one or more F-A-I-R-N-E-W-S investigations using the templates

F – A – I – R – N – E – W – S
EIGHT TESTS FOR FAIRNESS IN NEWS REPORTING

Fake facts

The first thing that we expect of news reporting is **accuracy** but news is sometimes inaccurate. Very occasionally facts and figures are **fabricated** – made up to fit the story – but there may also be **human error**: that is, the reporter may have been forgetful or careless, or there may have been a slip in communicating information to the news agency or radio/TV station. Whether the mistake is accidental or deliberate, it is still a mistake and it can still be unfair.

The 'F' test is one of the hardest for us. The difficulty with this test of fairness is that we don't always know whether the facts are correct. After all, we're reading, listening to or watching the news in order to get the facts! If a report contains mistakes, we have to rely on someone else who was at the scene or an expert on the matter to contact the media and set the matter straight. A good radio/TV station or newspaper will correct the mistakes and apologise but the media don't like doing this because it takes up time or space and it makes them look bad.

Some questions we ask for the 'F' test are:

■ Do we know whether the facts and figures are correct?

■ Do they seem to be correct?

■ How can we find out if they are correct?

■ If they're wrong, what can we do about fake facts?

Added-on answers

ASome news reporting goes further than giving the facts. The reporter or the presenter gives their **feelings** and **opinions** about what happened, based on their own **attitudes** and **assumptions**. They seem to want to tell us what they think should or should not have happened. In other words, they **add on answers** of their own and this makes it hard for us to make up our own minds. Yet good media have opinion pieces but keep them **separate** from news reporting.

Sometimes we see added-on answers in the **conclusion** to the news item but – because some people don't read, watch or listen to the end! – media often give us their answer at the beginning;

for example, in newspaper picture **captions and headlines** or radio/TV opening headlines. Often the caption or headline is giving added-on answers but the rest of the news item is factually correct and fair.

Some questions we need to ask for the 'A' test are:

■ Are there clues in the news item that facts and feelings have been muddled up or mixed together?

■ If so, what sense can we make of the news item?

■ What can we do about added-on answers?

Images and idioms

Good news is bad news! The media like conflicts and dramatic events. Media are businesses so – to make people read, listen and watch – they dramatise events in the images they show and the idioms (kinds of words) they choose. They tend to use very loaded words. This strong language strengthens the added-on answers.

Some questions we need to ask for the 'I' test are:

■ What kinds of words are used to describe the key players in the event? (For example, are they described as 'terrorists', 'militants', 'insurgents', 'freedom fighters' or 'protestors'?)

■ How are the key players shown? Do they seem to be like us?

■ On the radio or TV, what is the presenter's tone of voice like? If there is music or sound effects, what are they like?

■ On TV, what is the reporter's body language like?

■ What sense do we make of these images and idioms?

■ What can we do about images and idioms?

Removed from reality

Sometimes a news item is part of an ongoing story but sometimes it seems to come from nowhere. We're told about the action of an individual or group as if there were no background to it, as if they acted without reason. We don't know **why** they said or did something. In other words, the event is taken **out of context**. It's only **half the story** because **their story is missing**. It can be very **misleading** because **not** telling something is sometimes telling a lot!

Some questions we need to ask for the 'R' test are:

■ What happened before the person or group said or did what is reported in the news?

■ What might have happened further back in the past that has something to do with what is going on now?

■ What can we do about removal from reality?

N Nagging

Nagging could be defined as repeating the truth too often! When someone nags us, they may have a fair point but they make the point so much that we feel got at. They're criticising us and trying to change us, and they keep going on about it. Sometimes nagging makes us do the thing we're being nagged about even more.

The media sometimes nag: they go on about an individual, group or a country. This is called 'over-reporting' or 'excessive reporting'. It can have the same effects as nagging someone in everyday life.

Some questions we need to ask for the 'N' test are:

■ What effects does nagging have on the behaviour of the individual, group or country?

■ What effects does nagging have on the way that other people see the individual, group or country?

■ What can we do about such nagging?

E Exaggeration

Exaggeration is partly to do with the **emotive** images and idioms that the media use (see 'I'). By the choice of words and pictures, tone of voice and body language, the writer or presenter can make something seem **better or worse** than it really is.

A news item can also be exaggerated when part of what happened at the time is **not told**, just as a story is removed from reality when the background is not given. This is called '**selective reporting**' and it **distorts the truth** as much as fake facts (see 'F'). A news report can be exaggerated when **too much time or space** is given to one part of the story and **not enough time or space** is given to another part of the story. The news item is making it black and white when it may be shades

of grey. This makes the report **unbalanced**. For the 'E' test, we have to think about the news report **as a whole**.

Some questions we need to ask for the 'E' test are:

■ What seems left out of the news story?

■ Which parts of this story seem to have been over-emphasised?

■ What can we do about exaggeration?

W Winners and losers

In everyday life, we feel it's unfair when we're picked on, that is, when several people are doing something wrong but we're the only one who is criticised or punished for it. The media also pick on some individuals, groups or countries. We know that no one is all good or all bad yet sometimes the media present individuals, groups or countries as if they are goodies or baddies and not real people. They do this by not telling us either the good things that the baddies do or the bad things that the goodies do. In other words, the media make the players in the story into winners and losers.

Stereotypes like these are bad for everyone. Even stereotypes that seem good are bad because they stop us seeing the individuals, groups and countries as **real**. The stereotype of the winner also means that we might expect more of them than of the loser and we might judge them more harshly. This is called 'double standards'.

Some questions we need to ask for the 'W' test are:

■ Is the news report showing us well-rounded real people?

■ What can we do about the showing of winners and losers?

S Siding with one side

'S' is a challenging test because we have to make up our minds about the news **as a whole** and decide whether the reporter or presenter has favourites and whether they're biased. '**Bias**' means **taking sides** or putting a **spin** on the events: not being **fair and balanced**.

Some questions we need to ask for the 'S' test are:

■ Is there bias in the report – or is it fair and balanced?

■ What can we do about siding with one side?

F – A – I – R – N – E – W – S

Name   **Date**

Details of news report analysed

_____

F Fake facts

....

....

....

_____

A Added on answers

....

....

....

_____

I Images and idioms

....

....

....

_____

R Removed from reality

....

....

....

F – A – I – R – N – E – W – S

N Nagging

E Exaggeration

W Winners and losers

S Siding with one side

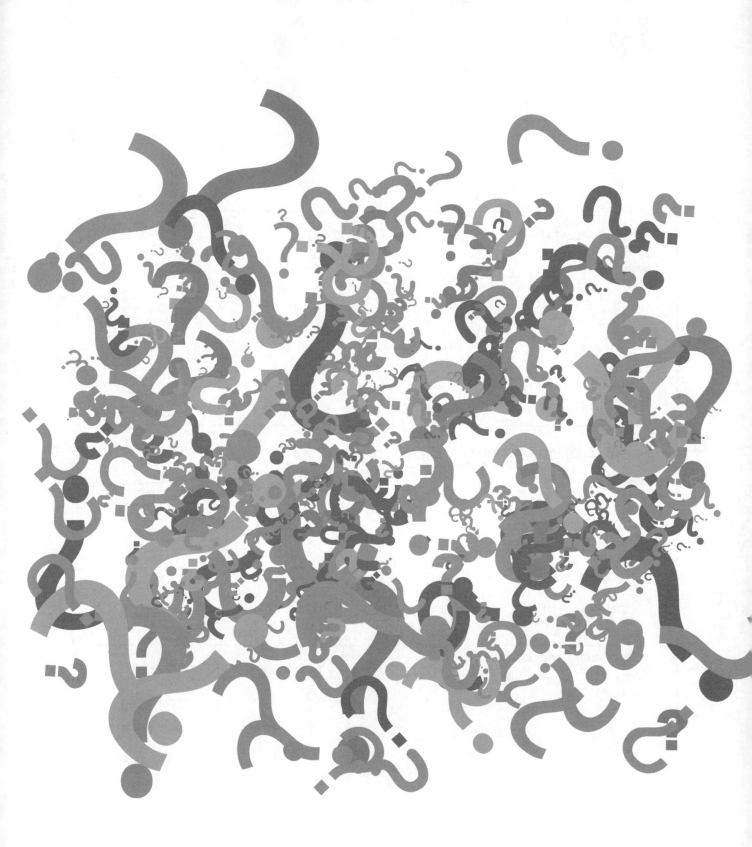

'THE ANSWERS AT THE BACK OF THE BOOK'

Finding the right word: a guide to the use of terms

The terms discussed here are those that appear in the exercise on page 11, introduced on page 10. These terms are subjective, dependent on context and capable of multiple definitions. These are answers rather than The Answer.

African Caribbean Afro-Caribbean Black British West Indian

'**African Caribbean**' technically means the same as 'Afro-Caribbean'. In the 1990s it replaced the term 'Afro-Caribbean' and was analogous to the American term 'African-American'.

'**Afro-Caribbean**' was used from the 1970s onwards – in preference to 'West Indian' – to refer to people of Caribbean heritage whose ancestors had originated in Africa. In highlighting African origins, this term recalls that many people of the Caribbean are descendants of slaves and it reclaims African culture as central to their identity.

'**Black British**' is the preferred term – at the Office of National Statistics – for British citizens of African or Caribbean ancestry, as well as those with ancestors elsewhere who consider themselves to be ethnically Black. It reclaims 'Black' and asserts 'British'.

The term 'West Indies', also known as the Caribbean (Islands), was used in the past to refer to British colonies. It was discarded because it reflected the erroneous view that British explorers had discovered India by travelling West. '**West Indian**' is not a nationality because there are several nations within the Caribbean. The use of 'West Indian' pre-dates the 1950s invited immigration into Britain of people from the West Indies. To use it today of individuals born in Britain – and their families and communities – would be to imply that they are not 'from here': it is usually disparaging in effect if not in intention.

anti-Muslim racism   Islamophobia

'**Anti-Muslim racism**' is sometimes used by academics to stress that they see anti-Muslim hostility as a form of racism. Conventionally, dictionary definitions of 'racism' have linked it to matters of 'race', that is, of physical appearance, particularly skin colour. There is a movement to apply 'racism' to more than antagonism towards people of different genotypes and to use it to cover antagonism in instances where the markers of difference are to do with culture, religion and language as well as physical appearance. 'Anti-Muslim racism' belongs under this broader definition.

'**Islamophobia**' is a fear of, hatred towards and prejudice against Islam and, by extension, Muslims. Eight components of Islamophobia were documented in the 1997 report of the Commission on British Muslims and Islamophobia *Islamophobia: A Challenge For Us All*. (A discussion of Islamophobia appears on pages 12-14)

anti-Judaism	antisemitism	antizionism

'**Anti-Judaism**' is the opposition to Judaism – the religion – exercised by another religion for theological reasons. It was endemic in medieval Christianity and led to physical violence, including murder. Elements of anti-Judaism remain amongst some Christian groups in the present and there are also traces of anti-Judaism amongst some Islamic groups.

'**Antisemitism**' is enmity towards Jews and was coined at the end of the 19th century, when theories of 'race' were being developed. Thus Jews were seen as a 'nation' or a 'race' apart. These ideas were reinforced under the Third Reich, in the Soviet Union and other regimes. Today antisemitism does not usually have a religious component.

'**Antizionism**' is opposition to the State of Israel and to the Zionist movement. It is most keenly expressed by some groups on the far left and the far right politically, and by some Islamic or Islamist groups. Antizionism may have a basis in antisemitism.

(A discussion of anti-Judaism, antisemitism and antizionism appears on pages 14-19).

arranged marriage	assisted marriage	forced marriage

In '**arranged marriage**' the parents of the bride and the groom agree on the marriage as the union of their two families and encourage the young man and the young woman to accept each other as their spouse. The bride and groom may or may not meet before the wedding. In cultures where marriages are arranged, young people generally accept that their parents have the wisdom and the good will to make the right choice. Sometimes parents consult their children before the marriage is arranged.

In an '**assisted marriage**', a man and a woman are introduced to one another – by their respective parents or another adult – with a view to their marriage. They may be encouraged to marry but their views are taken seriously and they maybe introduced to other prospective spouses.

In a '**forced marriage**', the views of the potential couple are not taken into account and indeed there is pressure upon them to marry. Force might be used.

assimilation	integration

'**Assimilation**' is based on the idea of making similar. It is the process of absorbing a minority group – particularly one that is newly arrived or newly formed – into a pre-existing community or society. This involves a significant loss of the distinctiveness of the newly arrived or newly formed group but relatively little change to the identity of the majority group. Indeed, the loss of distinctiveness is the key to membership of the majority group. 'Assimilation' is close in meaning to 'acculturation'.

'**Integration**' is based on the idea of making whole. It is the process whereby parts merge to form a whole, each receiving and contributing to the identity of the other.

Thus, assimilation is like soup and integration is like salad. But in practice 'assimilation' and 'integration' are often used synonymously.

coloured people	people of colour

'**Coloured people**' was a phrase for black and brown-skinned people, used both by those describing and by those being described. In its day, it was considered polite or mild as it avoided 'Black', which had negative connotations. It is now archaic and demeaning.

'**People of colour**' has emerged as an alternative to 'Black' in the USA and is widely used to refer to include African-Americans, Native Americans and Hispanic Americans.

community cohesion	social cohesion

'**Community cohesion**' is the state of stability, harmony and well being in a local community or society as a whole. As a series of social projects, it is an attempt to build or regenerate a shared vision for life; a commitment to the value of diversity; equal life chances; and strong relationships between members of the community or society.

'**Social inclusion**' is a policy initiative to tackle disadvantage and disaffection. It focuses on those who are seen to be or see themselves as excluded from society and not fully benefiting from its goods and services. In aiming to close the opportunity gap between the least advantaged groups and communities and the rest of society, it focuses on support for the most needy. It operates in domains that include education, employment and training, health and housing.

While their points of focus and concern are clearly linked, community cohesion and social inclusion are distinct; yet the two terms are often run together or even used interchangeably.

conservative	fundamentalist

'**Conservative**' means cautious and conventional. In social and educational policy, it connotes resistant to change and therefore opposing reform. Being conservative is usually identified with the political right wing and with social and religious movements that emphasise respect for tradition and authority.

'**Fundamentalist**' was coined in America towards the end of the nineteenth century to refer to churches and individuals who wished to maintain the 'fundamentals' of Christianity. Marked by a literal reading of scripture, fundamentalism insists that scripture was divinely revealed and that tradition has faithfully preserved this revelation in its entirety. It is therefore an anti-modernist movement that vigorously opposes the notion that religious teachings are the product of social context or the interaction between social context and divine revelation. It sees modernist trends as having corrupted the fundamentals of the faith and heralds a 'back to basics' movement. In the early days it was a mark of proud self-definition but in the course of time acquired negative associations. Today it is almost invariably used of religious leaders, groups and ideologies and may be ascribed *to* them by seldom *by* them of themselves. Numerically, fundamentalism is most apparent in Christian or Islamic groups. Fundamentalism sometimes manifests in political and social action. (Grahame Thompson's 'Five Features of Fundamentalism' – extremism, leader-fixation, aggression, sacrifice and endurance – are summarised on page 21).

disturbances	riots

A '**disturbance**' is a disorderly outburst in a public space that perturbs or agitates those who are not involved and causes stability – or the previously perceived stability – to be disrupted.

A '**riot**' is a public act of violence by an unruly crowd of people. It connotes the unrest and even turbulence of 'mob rule'.

Both disturbances and riots may occur as an act of – or take place in the context of – political or social protest. The media often use 'riot' when 'disturbance would be more fitting: this can further inflame the feelings of those protesting.

diversity	equality

In referring to human heterogeneity and to wide varieties of characteristics, qualities and behaviours, '**diversity**' is a term to be applied to a *collective* (such as a community, faith group or society as a whole) but it posits the uniqueness of *individuals*.

In mathematics and science '**equality**' means 'sameness'. However, no two *people* are the same. Thus, in human terms, 'equality' means having the same *value* and therefore worthy of the same consideration and respect. In educational practice, equality translates into equality of *opportunity* when everyone involved in a school or programme has equal access to the human and material resources they need. Because people are not identical and especially because people have unequal starting points, equality of opportunity can paradoxically involve unequal provision to achieve the aim of valuing people equally.

In educational and social policy, '**diversity**' and '**equality**' are two sides of the same coin: both take account of differences in factors such as aptitude or attainment, ethnicity, financial circumstances, gender, language, learning styles, religious affiliation and sexual orientation. However, they are not synonymous because 'equal' is not the same as 'same': equality is incomplete without a recognition of diversity and recognition of diversity should be accompanied by equality of respect. Differences should be recognised in a discriminating, but not discriminatory, way.

ethnic minority	minority ethnic

Stated simply, an '**ethnic minority**' is a group of people who are of different ethnicity from most people in the society in which they live. In practice, it is almost invariably a group that is more disadvantaged – or has less power in another sense – than the majority.

In recent years, '**minority ethnic**' has replaced 'ethnic minority' in some quarters – including the government and some local authorities: in 'minority ethnic', the noun 'minority' is, ungrammatically, used an adjective. The technical use is also slightly different in that the phrase needs to be followed by another noun, such as 'pupils' or 'communities'. 'Minority ethnic pupils' is a little less cumbersome than 'pupils from ethnic minorities' but is arguably dehumanising in tone. 'Black and minority ethnic' – especially when reduced to 'BME' – is very demeaning, albeit often part of official rhetoric. It is also nonsensical in that the 'and' implies that Black people are not part of an ethnic minority. It further lumps all minority groups together in a way that suggests that what they have in common is that they are not part of the majority.

extremist	fanatical	radical

'**Extremist**' is used of ideas and actions that appear hyperbolic to others and the use of the term implies a norm and deviation model. 'Extremist' is not usually a term used of the self and is characteristically negative. its use is relative as one person's extremist is another person's moderate.

The plain meaning of '**fanatical**' is characterised by intense devotion to and excessive enthusiasm for an idea, movement or cause. 'Fan', meaning an ardent supporter, is short for 'fanatic'. 'Fanatical' in the media connotes rabidity and there are usually associations with, or implications of, violence. As with 'extremist', the use is relative.

The meaning of '**radical**' relates to 'root'. In the 19th century in Western Europe, radicals advocated reforms more vigorously than liberals. Thus a radical movement is one that seeks to change things in their very essence. Recently the term 'radicalised' has been coined to describe the process whereby some Muslims become involved in social change and political action that for them expresses the essence of Islam.

faith	religion	spirituality

'**Faith**' is a personal belief or set of beliefs, sometimes contrasted with reason, suggesting that faith is groundless. It may or may not be part of a religion.

'**Religion**' – from the Latin for 'connect' – is a system of believing, behaving and belonging, that integrates a view of life and a way of life, and gives coherence to an individual's existence. It is a framework of belief in a supreme power, ethical codes, a body of texts, and patterns of worship, celebration and commemoration. 'Religion' is normally used in the context of 'organised religion', that is, a well-established organisation that has prescriptive and proscriptive elements.

'**Spirituality**' is a sense that there is more to life than meets the eye, that reality has a non-material dimension and that there is a something or someone greater than all of us. It recognises and responds to a meaning in existence that transcends any being or any situation. Spirituality may be agnostic, atheistic, dualistic, monotheistic, pantheistic or polytheistic.

Falklands	Malvinas

The '**Falklands**' – that is, the Falkland Islands – are an archipelago in the South Atlantic, east of the Strait of Magellan. Controlled by Great Britain since the 1830s, the islands are also claimed by Argentina and were occupied briefly by Argentinian troops in 1982 before being reoccupied by British forces. They are currently administered as a largely self-governing overseas territory of the United Kingdom.

The '**Malvinas**' – that is, *Las Islas Malvinas*, the Malvinas Islands – are an archipelago in the South Atlantic, east of the Strait of Magellan. Controlled by Great Britain since the 1830s, the islands are also claimed by Argentina and were occupied briefly by Argentinian troops in 1982 before being reoccupied by British forces. They are currently administered as a largely self-governing overseas territory of the United Kingdom.

In other words, Malvinas and Falklands are exactly the same place. The choice of name reflects the speaker's or writer's language and beliefs about the ownership of the islands.

freedom-fighter	insurgent	militant	terrorist

These four terms are very close in their literal meanings, with differences in their connotations and the language constituencies that use them. Media organisations have very specific guidelines on which to use and usually tend towards caution. They are, for example, reluctant to use 'terrorist' unless the word is specifically called for.

A '**freedom-fighter**' is an actor in an armed rebellion against a constituted authority, usually at a local level and on a relatively small scale, employing sabotage and harassment; it is a synonym for 'guerrilla'. 'Freedom' and 'rebellion' are contentious, however, as both factions in the conflict claim to be defending freedom: oppressors usually claim to be liberators, while freedom fighters usually become oppressors in the eyes of civilians. 'Freedom-fighter' is now used less commonly than in the 1960s and 1970s.

An '**insurgent**' is a member of a political party that rebels against an authority or established leadership, usually in a more coordinated way than a freedom-fighter. Insurgent forces typically constitute a private or alternative army.

The literal meaning of '**militant**' is belligerent or war-like and, as with freedom-fighters and insurgents, militants engage in violence as part of a declared struggle towards a political goal. Occasionally, 'militant' describes a soldier in combat as a member of a country's regular armed forces. The media often use 'militant' as an ostensibly neutral label for those who use violence without belonging to an established military.

A 'terrorist' is also one who systematically employs intimidation and physical violence to achieve political objectives. The defining characteristic of a terrorist is the use of civilian disguise in dress and behaviour, the operation in civilian areas and the targeting of civilians. Thus the Geneva Conventions do not protect terrorists in the way that soldiers in official armies are entitled to protection if captured by the enemy. An additional feature is the inspiration and stimulus to terrorism that derives from political or religious ideology. Furthermore, terrorists can achieve some of their aims by creating a climate of fear as part of their political, economic, religious, or ideological goals.

gender	sex

'Gender' refers to an individual's masculine or feminine status, which has biological components but is also socially constructed or culturally determined.

As well as shorthand for 'sexual activity', 'sex' refers to the properties that distinguish people on the basis of their reproductive roles. It is a biological given. However, 'sex' is colloquially used as a synonym for 'gender'.

In short, sex is either 'male' or 'female' and gender is 'femininity' or 'masculinity'.

Global South	Third World

'Third World' refers to the poorest regions of the world and is a synonym for 'undeveloped' or 'developing'. 'Third World' came into use in the 1960s, during the Cold War, to distinguish these regions from power blocs of the capitalist democratic 'First World' and the communist totalitarian 'Second World'. This problematically placed poor countries at the bottom of the hierarchy. Further, the term is nonsensical today since the Second World as a power bloc no longer exists.

Given that the most impoverished regions in the world are in the south, 'Global South' is the preferred descriptor: it makes no loaded judgements about the significance of these regions.

god	God

A 'god' refers to a supernatural being or personification of a cosmic force, who is the object of veneration. Sometimes 'god' is a synonym for 'idol' (see 'idol' below and the discussion on page 7). In some belief systems, there are more than one god, each being responsible for an aspect of reality.

In monotheistic belief systems, 'God' is the term for – or the name of – the one supernatural being.

Gypsy	Romany	Traveller

'Gypsy' is the most commonly understood label for an ethnic group of nomadic – or formerly nomadic – people. 'Gypsy' is a misnomer because it is a variant of 'Egyptian', the group being mistakenly believed to have originated in Egypt: they are more likely to have originated in northern India. 'Gypsy' has long had negative associations. However the term has recently been reclaimed – but only with a capital 'G'.

'Romany' (sometimes 'Romani') is the Indic language of a nomadic people that migrated to Europe and elsewhere. It is also a name for the people themselves (plural: 'Romanies') and is a self-definition. Government terminology currently favours 'Roma' but this should be restricted to the collective and not applied to individuals; for example, a 'Romany child' rather than a 'Roma child'.

'Traveller' is a replacement for 'Gypsy' that removes the pejorative connotations but its use is often confusing because others are travellers, for example, commercial travellers and New Age Travellers.

idol	image	symbol

An 'idol' is an effigy or representation of a deity – and, in some religious traditions, an *embodiment* of the deity – that is the focus of veneration. Typically, idols are associated with polytheism (see the discussion on page 7).

In everyday speech, an 'image' is the impression that a person or object presents. In visual art, it is a physical likeness or representation of a person or thing, or a thought or feeling that is given visible form. In religions, it is a *mental* representation of a deity or a theological precept, as in 'an image of the afterlife'.

A 'symbol' is something concrete and visible that, by association or convention, represents something abstract and invisible. It differs from a sign or label in that the form of a symbol is not arbitrary but implies or conveys the essence of the meaning, beyond its immediate sense. Thus, a dove is a dove but can also be symbol for peace.

Indian sub-continent	South Asia

'**The Indian subcontinent**' is the peninsula bound by the Himalayas to the north and east, the Arabian Sea and the Bay of Bengal to the south, and the Kush mountains to the west. This region includes Bangladesh, Bhutan, India, Nepal and Pakistan. It sometimes also includes Myanmar, Sri Lanka (an island) and part of the disputed territory currently controlled by China.

'**South Asia**' also refers to the peninsula bound by the Himalayas, the Arabian Sea and the Bay of Bengal, and the Kush mountains. It is a preferred term because, in not referring to specific countries, it does not privilege India. This is particularly important because of the disputes about borders with India.

interfaith	multifaith

'**Interfaith**' describes a relationship or interface between faiths (or religions).

'**Multifaith**' describes a community or society in which one or more faiths (or religions) are present.

Islamic	Islamist	Muslim

'**Islamic**' is an adjective derived from 'Islam'. It applies to aspects of Islam (such as 'Islamic jurisprudence'), to practices in keeping with Islam (such as 'Islamic dress') and to societies that embody the principles of Islam. It is not used of individuals or families.

'**Islamist**' is of recent coinage. Islam is more than a religion in the sense that it is often understood in the modern world: Islam influences and governs all aspects of life and has legal and political aspects. Islamist beliefs stress that Islam is a political system that informs legal, economic and social initiatives. 'Islamist' may therefore be used to describe a person or organisation that engages Islamic religious precepts in a political ideology or movement, characteristically inclining towards the more conservative interpretations of such precepts. 'Islamist' has come to mean – especially when used by opponents – an antagonism to liberalism and modernity in Western countries, as well as to some Muslim societies and governments. Frequently, the media use 'Islamist', 'fundamentalist' and 'violence' in the same breath. 'Islamist' – and 'Islamism' – have become problematic terms and should be used with caution.

'**Muslim**' is an adjective derived from 'Islam'. It applies to individuals and families who are adherents of Islam or relate to the Islamic heritage.

Israel	Israel-Palestine	Palestine

'**Israel**' is an area in western Asia, at the eastern end of the Mediterranean Sea, which was the homeland of the Jewish people in ancient times and from which the majority was exiled in 70 CE. A Jewish republic-called the 'State of Israel' – was declared in 1948, following international initiatives, including the Balfour Declaration of 1917, a United Nations resolution in 1947 and the end of the British Mandate of Palestine. 'Israel' is also a term traditionally used by Jews for the Jewish community worldwide.

'**Palestine**' derives from a Roman name for a region in western Asia. In the last two millennia, many definitions of 'Palestine' have been in use and the borders have shifted more than once. Following their final defeat in 135 CE of the Jewish uprising against Roman occupation, the Romans sought to remove traces of former Jewish sovereignty: they renamed the Jewish homeland and other areas they had conquered 'Syria Palestina' or 'Palestina'. The name passed into English and other European languages as 'Palestine'. Over the centuries this region changed hands several times and was part of the Ottoman Empire for 400 years. Following World War I, part of 'Palestine' came under the caretaker government of the British Mandate, Britain having indicated its intention to create a national homeland for the Jewish people in Palestine. During the Mandate, the British designated the region east of the River Jordan as an Arab state and named it 'Transjordan'; it later became the Hashemite Kingdom of Jordan. Following the war of 1948 between Israel and surrounding Arab countries, Jordan occupied an area west of the River Jordan (usually referred to as the 'West Bank') and Egypt the Gaza Strip.

'**Palestinian**' can refer to a Jew born in the region during the Ottoman Empire or the British Mandate of Palestine. But it is much more frequently used of the Arabs who live there, and those who are related to them but live elsewhere: most are Muslim but there are also Christian and other communities. Some Arabs who live in Israel and are Israeli citizens call themselves 'Palestinian' rather than 'Israeli Arabs'.

In the Six Day War of 1967, the West Bank and Gaza were captured by Israel. This stimulated nationalist aspirations on the part of Palestinian Arabs. Since that time, several peace initiatives between Arab and Israeli representatives resulted in limited autonomy for Palestinian Arabs in the West Bank. In 2005 Israel withdrew from Gaza and handed it to Palestinian control.

The meaning of 'Palestine' and the precise area to which it refers are both changing and controversial. For example, there is, as yet, no country officially called 'Palestine' but there are Palestinian territories in the West Bank and Gaza. Some Arab groups consider Israel to be part of Palestine and do not recognise it as a country in its own right.

There is no such place as 'Israel-Palestine' but it is impossible to speak of one of these regions without reference to the other. Thus, the term refers to the relationship between the Israel and the Palestinian territories. Given that there are disputed land claims, it also has the benefits of neutrality as neither area or country is privileged.

lady	woman

As both 'lady' and 'woman' mean 'adult female human', the choice between them may be a matter of convention or may be influenced by gender politics.

'**Lady**' is generally a polite, delicate or even honourific form, as in 'ladies' night', 'the ladies' (toilet) and a male or female hairdresser referring to a client as 'my lady'. It might be used satirically, as in the tongue-in-cheek 'Now look here, lady!'

By contrast with 'lady', '**woman**' seems basic or ordinary. However, in recent decades it has been reclaimed to connote strength and realism. This is conveyed no more clearly that in designating feminist initiatives as 'the women's movement'. Here 'woman' is asserted as independent, confident, decisive and unpretentious.

Although 'woman' is now the norm, it's best to check with the adult female human concerned!

political correctness	political correctness gone mad

'**Political correctness**' (or 'PC') was first used in the 1970s, as a result of the liberal movements – and especially the student demonstrations – of the late 1960s; it entered everyday speech in the 1980s. It is the practice of using language in harmony with liberal or radical opinion by avoiding or expunging words and expressions that might – or might be perceived to – offend or disadvantage social minorities; in particular, words and expressions that have or might have racist, sexist or homophobic overtones. Political correctness – although not always under that name – influences public policy and colours the discourse of national and local government, and the voluntary sector: while usually a linguistic phenomenon, it also extends to political ideology and practice. It is a form of cultural Marxism in its focus on power and powerlessness.

Some politicians, policy-makers, journalists and others who are opposed to some or all aspects of political correctness use the expression '**political correctness gone mad**' when they feel that the constraints on language are excessive or unnecessary. 'Political correctness gone mad' seems to have a strong and a weak form, both of which see political correctness as a form of insanity.

In its *weak or surface form*, it asserts that political correctness is too extreme or too extensive. It cites policy statements that make people fearful of saying or writing the 'wrong' thing. It ridicules instances of people being criticised or even disciplined for innocently using everyday words and idioms, unaware that they had an entirely different meaning in days gone by. It stresses that language is dynamic and interactive, and meanings change over time (for example, 'awful' once spelled 'aweful' and meaning 'awesome'). It further claims that political correctness is often *historically* incorrect in ascribing historic associations of at least some of these words. It points out that such usage could only offend if the person describing, the person being described and those listening to or reading the description were aware of an earlier meaning and, further, if that earlier meaning continued to resonate in the language.

In its *strong or deep form*, 'political correctness gone mad' is really a way of saying 'political correctness gone *bad*': it is not simply that political correctness should be held in check; it should be done away with. It denounces the blame culture that it sees as accompanying political correctness, and leads to bitter accusations or even legal trials. It considers that western society has lost a sense of balance and proportion. It further bewails what it deems to be a culture in which increasingly large numbers of people feel obliged to perceive, and present themselves, as victims. Its main bone of contention, however, is concerned with the loss of freedom: in this, it cites freedom of speech as the hallmark of a democratic, progressive and civilised society.

pupils with special needs	SEN pupils

'**Pupils with special needs**' usually means 'pupils with special *educational* needs', in other words, pupils whose special needs relate to their educational progress. Such pupils are usually understood to be those who have a significantly greater degree of difficulty in learning than the majority of their age group. Their needs may be related to cognition, perception, mobility, speech, emotional health and social behaviour – or a combination of these factors. In some contexts, the language is of 'extra needs', 'additional needs', 'disabilities' and 'difficulties'.

'**SEN pupils**' – short for 'special educational needs pupils' – is understandably tempting to use as it is not too cumbersome, but it is problematic. The use of 'SEN' as an adjective defines the pupils by their SEN-ness. This is an example of a small difference in wordage yielding a huge difference in meaning.

racial	racist

'**Racial**' is the adjective derived from 'race' that describes the physical characteristics of a particular human race. It also inherits the problematic nature of 'race'. There are those who argue that human races do not exist because there is only one human race. Given that 'race' is perceived as a physical phenomenon, they cite biological findings – along with plain observation of life – to the effect that the two people of different 'races' can reproduce. They see race as an arbitrary, socially constructed category. They also focus on spurious studies of genetics from the 19th century onwards that posited different races; that asserted that inherent biological differences between human races determine cultural or individual achievement; and claimed to be able to identity and isolate their characteristics. They further note that such pseudo-scientific studies were used in the 20th century as a theoretical basis for the most grotesque racist policies and practices in history-genocide.

'**Racist**' also derives from 'race'. By contrast with 'racial', the word 'racist' is not problematic but racist attitudes and behaviour palpably are. Racism is a body of beliefs and behaviours that is not only based on the premise that there are separate races with inherent differences but on the notion of a hierarchy of races – with one's own race (that is, that of the racist) being superior to all others. Racism propagates and justifies unjust and inhumane treatment of so-called inferior races and, in its extreme form, attempts their extermination.

resistance	revolt	revolution

'**Resistance**', meaning active opposition to policies and procedures of a regime and to the regime itself, is frequently the name of a secret organisation to overthrow an occupying force. It uses subterfuge and sabotage, and sometimes directs physical violence against the personnel of the occupying power.

'**Revolt**' can be simply a refusal to accept authority in an individual's personal situation that might manifest in the flouting of social norms. It can equally be a form of organised opposition to authority or a conflict in which one party aims to wrest control from another.

A '**revolution**' is a rapid and far-reaching shift in thought and behaviour, generated from within a society, often resulting in drastic changes in culture, such as in the industrial revolution, the sexual revolution and the cultural revolution. It usually stimulates the renewal or replacement of social or political institutions and might cause the overthrow of a government by the governed. A revolution might be violent – as in France in 1978 and Russia in 1917 – but there are also bloodless revolutions.

you	you people

'**You**' is the simple way of addressing another person or persons. Whether sensitive or insensitive, polite or impolite, angry or calm, it respects the humanity and the individuality of the person or persons being spoken to.

By contrast, '**you people**' is invariably derogatory and dehumanising. It paints the person or persons addressed into a picture of a group – that may not be named – that the speaker opposes or even hates. It denies the addressee's individuality by implying that 'you' are a committed member of that group, are acting as its representative and need to justify its actions or even its very existence. The attitude to the group in question is essentially 'ist', that is, racist, sexist and so on. It is a very denial of the premise and proposition of *What do we tell the children?*

You may not be people *like us* but you are *people*, like us.

CREDITS AND REFERENCES

Credits

The photo on page on 14 was taken by Suki Dhanda in 2002 and is part of the 'Shopna and her friends' series, which can be seen at www.sukidhanda.com

All efforts have been made to trace the sources of images 1-13 (pages 37-44) but with no success. We apologise to the artists and will be glad to publish acknowledgements if they are forthcoming.

The twelve strategies for 'Telling Tales' (pages 48-53) have been abridged and amended from text in Angela Wood and Robin Richardson, *Inside Stories: wisdom and hope for changing worlds*, Trentham Books, 1992. The following stories have been taken, with some amendments, from the same publication: *The Stonecutter* (page 70), *Whoever Comes This Way* (pages 73-74) and *Five Journeys* (pages 75-76).

References

Judith Bumpus, Saudis see how their sisters live, *The Times*, 10 May 2006

T. S. Eliot (1934), Choruses from the Rock, *Complete Poems and Plays: 1909-1950*, New York: Harcourt Brace, 1980

Timothy Garton Ash, What we call Islam is a mirror in which we see ourselves, *The Guardian*, 15 September 2005

Robert Graves, 'The Cool Web' in Philip Larkin (ed.) *The Oxford Book of Twentieth Century English Verse*, OUP 1973/90. Original in either *Collected Poems 1965* or *Over the Brazier*, both published by A. P. Watt and Son

Gotthold Ephraim Lessing, *Nathan the Wise* (translated from the German by Edward Kemp), Nick Hern Books, London, 2003

Rageh Omaar, *Only Half of Me: being a Muslim in Britain*, Viking Books, 2006

Yossi Sarid, Now The Fruit Will Wait Till It Rots, *HaAretz*, 17 July 2006

Leonard Swidler, Ground Rules for Inter-religious, Inter-cultural Dialogue, *Journal of Ecumenical Studies*, 1983

Amir Tahri,'We Don't Do God, We Do Palestine And Iraq, *The Sunday Times*, 12 February 2006

Grahame Thompson, *What is fundamentalism?* www.opendemocracy.net, 9 March 2006 'Aspects of fundamentalism-a selection of links' can be found at http://www.insted.co.uk/fundamentalism.pdf

Susan Varley, *Badger's Parting Gifts*, HarperCollins, London, 1992.

Judith Viorst, 'If we can't promise, *The Washington Post*, 11 September 2002

Denis Wood, Ward L. Kaiser and Bob Abramms, *Seeing Through Maps: Many Ways to See the World*, ODT Inc., Amherst (Massachusetts), 2006

Other Sources

The '3Ds' (demonisation; double standards; delegitimisation) speech by Minister Natan Sharansky, Head of the Israeli Delegation to the OSCE Conference on Anti Semitism Berlin, 28-29 April 2004, can be found at www.mfa.gov.il (under 'Antisemitism/Holocaust').

The 'Golden Rule Across the World's Religions' project, initiated by Paul McKenna" in Canada can be seen at www.scarboromissions.ca

Commission on British Muslims and Islamophobia (set up by The Runnymede Trust in 1997) produced two reports: *Islamophobia: a challenge for us all* (1997) and *Islamophobia: issues, challenges and action* (2004) published by Trentham Books. Further details are at www.insted.co.uk

Simon Wiesenthal Center and the Museum of Tolerance www.wiesenthal.com, *Digital Terrorism and Hate* (interactive CD-Rom) May 2006

Runnymede Trust, *Commission on the Future of Multi-Ethnic Britain* (the Parekh Report) Profile Books, 2000

The Runnymede Trust, *A Very Light Sleeper: the persistence and dangers of antisemitism*, London, Runnymede, 1994

Report of the All Party Inquiry Into Antisemitism, The Stationery Office, London, 7 September 2006; also available at http://thepcaa.org/Report.pdf